This is Peter Lewis at his best! Peter ...
Christlikeness through the w... ...
clear, compelling, biblically ri...
meaningful quotes that reflect ...
reading. *Becoming Christlike* not ...
like Christ – we learn the path to ... ... it down.
Neither will you.
Becky Manley Pippert, speaker and au... ... Out of the Salt Shaker and into the World

Christlikeness is the ultimate goal of the Christian life, produced not merely by imitating Christ, but by Christ being himself within his regenerate people. His life imparted to us becomes the source of new appetites, new empowerment and new fruitfulness. Peter Lewis helpfully explores the source and the outworking of this in both personal and corporate life, in good times and in bad, in the light and in the dark, when God seems close and when he seems distant. Full of memorable illustrations, this book will help both the newest believer and the most mature disciple.
Charles Price, Teaching Pastor, The People's Church, Toronto

This is a powerful presentation of what it means for a Christian to be Christlike. Peter Lewis roots his message deeply in Scripture. In his development of his theme, he connects with a remarkable range of Christian thinking and human experience. The whole book communicates a crucial call to a different way of living. But Peter Lewis shows compellingly that the demands of such a life are more than fully matched by the resources God has made available. Read what is written here with an open heart, and be prepared to be challenged and changed by it.
Ian Randall, author and Senior Research Fellow, Spurgeon's College, London

Drawing on a lifetime of ministry experience, Peter Lewis has written a concise, clear and comprehensive theology of the Christian life. With a blend of faithful exegesis, pithy quotations and personal anecdotes, he reminds us that God's great purpose is that we should be transformed into the likeness of the Lord Jesus Christ. Readers will be encouraged to rejoice afresh in all that Christ has done for them, challenged to pursue holiness in every area of their lives, and inspired to look forward to the eternal glory to come. It would be impossible to read this book without repenting afresh and seeking God's help to live a new life by the power of his Holy Spirit.

John Stevens, National Director, Fellowship of Independent Evangelical Churches

Filled with fascinating stories and anecdotes, focused on a wonderful theme and founded on glorious biblical truth, you will find great enrichment in reading Peter Lewis's delightful book.

Terry Virgo, founder, Newfrontiers

PETER LEWIS

BECOMING CHRISTLIKE

INTER-VARSITY PRESS
36 Causton Street, London SW1P 4ST, England
Email: ivp@ivpbooks.com
Website: www.ivpbooks.com

First published 2016

British Library Cataloguing-in-Publication Data
A catalogue record for this book is available from the British Library.

ISBN: 978–1–78359–437–5
ebook ISBN: 978–1–78359–487–0

Set in Dante 12/15pt
Typeset in Great Britain by CRB Associates, Potterhanworth, Lincolnshire
Printed in Great Britain by Ashford Colour Press Ltd, Gosport, Hampshire

*Inter-Varsity Press publishes Christian books that are true to the Bible and that
communicate the gospel, develop discipleship and strengthen the church for its mission
in the world.*

*IVP originated within the Inter-Varsity Fellowship, now the Universities and Colleges
Christian Fellowship, a student movement connecting Christian Unions in universities
and colleges throughout Great Britain, and a member movement of the International
Fellowship of Evangelical Students. Website: www.uccf.org.uk. That historic association
is maintained, and all senior IVP staff and committee members subscribe to the UCCF
Basis of Faith.*

This book is dedicated to my beloved wife Valerie,
who has lived Christlikeness in our home for so many years

Contents

Series preface   ix
Foreword   xi
Preface   xv

Part 1: The source of Christlikeness
1. Our place in God's eternal plan   3
2. We have been set apart for God   15
3. We are united to Christ for ever   27

Part 2: The model of Christlikeness
4. The down-to-earth God   41
5. This is your life: the Sermon on the Mount   51
6. The Suffering Servant and suffering Christians   63

Part 3: The helps to Christlikeness
7. The Spirit of God   77
8. The Word of God   91
9. The place of prayer   103
10. The people of God   113

Part 4: The contradictions of Christlikeness
11. Facing the contradictions in our society   125
12. Facing the contradictions within ourselves   135

Part 5: The triumph of Christlikeness

13. The return with Christ   149
14. Christlike at last!   161

Notes   173
Keswick Ministries   179

Keswick Foundations: Series preface

*Our prayer was for deep, clear, powerful teaching, which
would take hold of the souls of the people, and
overwhelm them, and lead them to a full, definite and
all-conquering faith in Jesus.*

This simple but profound prayer, expressed by Thomas
Harford-Battersby as he reported on the 1880 Keswick Convention, explains why hundreds of thousands of Christians the
world over have been committed to the Keswick movement.
The *purpose* is nothing other than to see believers more wholeheartedly committed to Jesus Christ in every area of life,
and the *means* the faithful, clear and relevant exposition of
God's Word.

All around the world, the Keswick movement has this
purpose and this means. Whether it is to proclaim the gospel,
to encourage discipleship, to call for holiness, to urge for
mission, to long for the Spirit's empowering or to appeal
for unity – hearing God's Word in Scripture is central to fulfilling these priorities. (More information about Keswick
Ministries is found at the end of this book.)

Keswick Foundations is a series of books that introduce the
priority themes that have shaped the Keswick movement,
themes which we believe continue to be essential for the
church today. By God's grace, for 140 years the movement has
had an impact across the globe, not only through Conventions

large and small, but also through a range of media. Books in the Keswick Foundations series provide biblical, accessible and practical introductions to basic evangelical essentials that are vital for every Christian and every local church.

Our prayer for these books is the same as that expressed by Harford-Battersby – that by his Spirit, God's Word will take hold of our souls, leading us to an all-conquering faith in Jesus Christ, which will send us out to live and work for his glory.

Foreword

I remember the evening vividly: a frail old man, walking stick in hand and supported by a friend, slowly climbing the steps to the Keswick Convention platform and onwards to the lectern. By this time in his life he had spoken on every continent of the world, to multiple thousands in baseball stadia, to hundreds in church buildings of every denomination, to congregations gathered under trees, at many student missions, as well as to many small groups. He had been named in *Time* magazine's '100 most influential people' in 2005, awarded the CBE in the Queen's New Year's honours list the following year, and considered one of the foremost global leaders of evangelicalism in the twentieth century. He had written over fifty books and preached thousands of sermons. And as he stood to give the final address of his long career as a preacher and teacher, this is what John Stott said at Keswick in 2009:

> I want to share with you where my mind has come to rest as I approach the end of my pilgrimage on earth, and it is – God wants his people to become like Christ. Christlikeness is the will of God for the people of God.

In addressing this most significant purpose of God for every Christian, John Stott was returning to a theme that has been part of the DNA of the Keswick movement worldwide since its earliest days. And it remains a core theme which needs to be proclaimed and modelled today. Stott opened with three basic texts to demonstrate the biblical basis for the call to Christlikeness.

First, God has predestined his people to be conformed to the image of his Son: that is, to become like Jesus. 'For those God foreknew he also predestined to be conformed to the image of his Son, that he might be the firstborn among many brothers and sisters' (Romans 8:29). The mission of the Lord Jesus, conceived in an eternity past, was nothing other than to restore the image, to overturn the disastrous effects of the fall and to restore within us the original divine image.

Second, God has provided the Holy Spirit, by whom we are being transformed into the image of Jesus himself. 'And we all, who with unveiled faces contemplate the Lord's glory, are being transformed into his image with ever-increasing glory, which comes from the Lord, who is the Spirit' (2 Corinthians 3:18).

Third, while many aspects of our future home in heaven are not clear, one thing is certain: we will be like Christ. 'Dear friends, now we are children of God, and what we will be has not yet been made known. But we know that when Christ appears, we shall be like him, for we shall see him as he is' (1 John 3:2). We will be with him and like him for all eternity.

So from the perspective of past, present and future, Scripture teaches us that this is God's purpose for every believer. We have been predestined for this in God's plans, we have been equipped for this by God's Spirit, and we will finally be like Christ on that final day. Nothing in life is more important.

This matters, because today it is widely agreed that holiness is a neglected priority of the modern church. It is for this reason that the Keswick movement wants once again to bring this theme to the front of the stage, and why it appears centrally in our strapline: 'Hearing God's Word, becoming like God's Son, serving God's mission'. This is God's loving and sovereign purpose for his people. And we must add that, in an age when people long for authenticity, there is no doubt that, for many non-Christians, the credibility of Christian witness often rests upon the integrity of the Christian believer. The watching world needs both to hear the gospel and to see that gospel embodied in the lives of Jesus' followers.

A concern for holiness has been the sustained heartbeat of the Keswick movement. It is disappointing that people caricature the present Keswick movement as being locked into a particular view of holiness (sometimes called 'the Keswick view'), when for the past fifty years the position taken on Keswick platforms has been entirely mainstream evangelical teaching, with which few believers could disagree. And when, in the past, there might have been differing views about how holiness could be achieved, there was far more nuancing in the teaching than some critics have allowed for. There were various vigorous debates about holiness at the time when Keswick started. Some Christians seemed to get worryingly close to the idea of sinless perfection, and others seemed to suggest that a crisis moment could secure a condition of Christlikeness, almost implying that no personal struggle or effort was needed from then on. (Both of these ideas have been rejected by the Keswick movement, of course, but you still hear the criticism, even in respectable journals, suggesting that this remains the Keswick position. May we say here: it does not!)

For many years the emphasis of the Keswick movement has been on the call for steady life transformation and growth in Christlikeness, but there has always been room at the Convention for 'preaching for a decision', when individuals hear God's Word, sense the Spirit's leading, and commit themselves more wholeheartedly to live for Christ. Such moments of focused intention are not crises that somehow achieve a higher level of spiritual experience, but are often manifestations of the power of God's Word and Spirit in provoking renewed repentance and faith, and a realization of the vital importance of living more fully under the lordship of Christ.

The Keswick movement has been governed by clear priorities. First, as Stott taught in his final public address at Keswick, God's purpose is that his people should become like his Son. Christlikeness is the will of God for the people of God, and this message must once again take centre stage. Second, we must continually examine the Scriptures to understand how this calling is to be worked out. The overriding concern must be to live according to the truth of God's Word. And third, our concern must be not only for correct theology, but for practical holiness, expressing day by day what Christlikeness looks like in a secular world.

For this reason, it is a special joy to introduce the book that you now hold in your hands. Peter Lewis combines the qualities of careful Bible exposition, practical and pastoral application, and a life lived for the Lord Jesus Christ, whom he here proclaims so eloquently. The theme of this book could not be more significant, and Keswick Ministries is delighted to add this inspirational title to its Foundations series.

Jonathan Lamb
CEO and minister-at-large
Keswick Ministries

Preface

As we've just seen, in his last address at Keswick Convention John Stott chose the subject of 'Christlikeness', a subject 'where my mind has come to rest', he said, as he prepared to leave this world. I have been asked to write a book that focuses on Christlikeness, which I gladly do since Christ has been the centre and inspiration of my ministry and writing for nearly fifty years now.

All over the world 'Keswick' is a name that is synonymous with evangelical faith and a serious desire for holiness. The Bible has a whole vocabulary to denote becoming more like God, including holiness, sanctification, righteousness, godliness, obedience and so on, but the term 'Christlike' has one great advantage alongside these. It ensures that we cannot easily become abstract or formal or legalistic, because it gathers them all up in the most beautiful and momentous life that ever was lived.

God entered our human story as one of us, immersed himself in our world of rebellion and sin, injustice and pain, and in an unparalleled act of redemption by his atoning death and glorious resurrection, opened the way into the future of God for millions. Since then his Spirit has moved in countless hearts, including our own, bringing us to a new understanding, humbling us in repentance, and raising us to joy and confidence in the justification of Christ. Now sanctification, as growth in holiness, obedience and love, can only be a God-sustained reaction and response to what his Son has done for us:

Were the whole realm of nature mine,
That were an offering far too small;
Love so amazing, so divine,
Demands my life, my soul, my all.[1]

This book is an introduction to the Bible's teaching on this.

In Part 1 we discover the biblical foundations of our subject. First, we examine the eternal plan of God to make a race of people who would bear his image and share his future, and we see that fulfilled in Christ and his people. Second, we see the decisive action of God in history and our own lives, setting his people apart for himself, and its lifelong implications. Third, we see our union with Christ as the sphere in which all this, and the entire course of our salvation, takes place.

In Part 2 we consider what becoming Christlike looks like in any age by taking Jesus as the model for us all. We consider his incarnation, the marvel of his grace in becoming one of us, the extent of his involvement with us and what it says to us in our day-to-day lives in our fallen, needy world. We look more closely at the Sermon on the Mount to see what revolutionary living is like and our own potential for such living. Finally, we examine the cost of Christlikeness in a world at war with God as we consider the suffering of Christ and the sufferings of the persecuted church today and are prepared for the challenges of Christ-centred living in a self-centred age.

Part 3 takes us to the main 'helps' we have in this. First, we have the Holy Spirit whom Jesus promised would be with us.

He, the Holy Spirit, is first and foremost, because without his activity and blessing none of the other helps would 'work' for us. Without him the Bible would be barren, prayer would have no promise, and the people of God would have no attraction for us. But by the work of the Spirit all these become the mainstay of our Christian lives, deepening the image of God and Christlikeness in us all.

Part 4 urges us to face the contradictions of Christlikeness around us and within us. These involve the discouragement and defiance we meet in the world when we commend Christ, and the power of temptation to attract and even seduce us into activity that is in direct contradiction with our life in Christ. I have chosen sexual temptation as my main example, for obvious reasons.

Part 5 reminds us that after all our struggles and experiences, our inadequacy and our hope, the last word is 'Yes' and 'Amen' in Christ. Finally, we look toward the Second Coming of Christ, what it means for our world and what it means for us: Christlike at last.

Lastly, I want to record my sincere thanks to Eleanor Trotter, my editor at IVP, who has guided me through the process of writing this book 'with great patience and careful instruction'; Kath Stanton, my copy-editor, who has minutely corrected the manuscript and curbed my preacher's prose; and Elizabeth McQuoid and the Keswick editorial/publications board who first asked me to write on this subject.

Part 1
The source of Christlikeness

1

Our place in God's eternal plan

One of the most profound and agitated questions of our time is this: 'Is there a purpose to life, to mine or anyone else's?' Can I have any freedom if I believe that there is a plan, and can I have any real peace or satisfaction if I believe that there isn't? Very often the answer is that there is no plan, no purpose, no ultimate goal to human life. But most people wish there were. Our philosophy says one thing, but our longings say another.

For many, the good news of Christ is quickly dismissed as too good to be true. The evangelist and theologian Michael Green recalled a wine-tasting evening hosted by Christians to reach out to the community. As people spoke about their faith, a woman professor leaned over to Michael and whispered, 'You know, I don't believe any of this.' Michael replied, 'Yeah, I know, but wouldn't you like to?' With that remark, tears welled up in the woman's eyes. Her head told her 'no', but her heart yearned to hear 'yes'.[1] The very fact that she was at such a gathering indicated that she was aware of this tension and that she needed to pursue it.

A crazy building

A few years ago the Christian apologist Ravi Zacharias visited the Wexner Center for the Arts on the campus of Ohio State University. When you enter the building, you encounter:

> stairways that go nowhere, pillars that hang from the ceiling without touching the floor, and angled surfaces configured to create a sense of vertigo. The architect, we are duly informed, designed this building to reflect life itself – senseless and incoherent – and the 'capriciousness of the rules that organize the built world'.[2]

When the rationale was explained to Ravi Zacharias, he had just one question for the guide: *'Did he do the same with the foundation?'*[3]

The point, of course, was that the architect would not have dreamed of putting his philosophy into real practice, because actually the rules of 'the built world' were not capricious. There was such a thing as purpose, order and design that worked, and to ignore it would be fatal. Here there was a philosophy above the ground that clashed with the reality below ground!

The message of the Bible is that life is not an accident and God is not capricious. God does have a plan, a plan that centres on Jesus and includes each one of us.

Jesus and the plan of God

Jesus was profoundly aware of God in his life and of God's plan for his life. His relationship to God his Father was unique, and his Father's plan for his life was unique. His understanding grew with the years, for as he studied the Scriptures, he saw himself and his life's work as the Holy Spirit unfolded his destiny:

> He went to Nazareth, where he had been brought up, and on the Sabbath day he went into the synagogue, as was his custom. He stood up to read, and the scroll of the prophet Isaiah was handed to him. Unrolling it, he found the place where it is written:
>
> 'The Spirit of the Lord is on me,
>   because he has anointed me
>   to proclaim good news to the poor.
> He has sent me to proclaim freedom for the prisoners
>   and recovery of sight for the blind,
> to set the oppressed free,
>   to proclaim the year of the Lord's favour.'
>
> Then he rolled up the scroll, gave it back to the attendant and sat down. The eyes of everyone in the synagogue were fastened on him. He began by saying to them, 'Today this scripture is fulfilled in your hearing.'
> (Luke 4:16–21)

For centuries the prophets had said that God would come and establish his rule of righteousness and peace on the earth. Jesus now announced that the waiting time was over, the kingdom of God was at hand and the future was here. With *him*!

He knew that his public ministry had to begin by standing alongside sinners in the waters of John's 'baptism of repentance for the forgiveness of sins' (Matthew 3:1, 13–15; Mark 1:4), even though he was the one man on earth who had no sins needing repentance and forgiveness. Throughout the ministry that followed he would be looking to the Father and listening to the Spirit, doing all he did in perfect harmony with the divine will which would guide and impel him (John 5:19–20; 6:38–40). This was his Father's plan: a plan drawn up in love, one that would not be allowed to fail, one that would issue in the everlasting joy of millions (John 6:37–40; 12:23–33).

But it would involve a great cost. His sacrificial death had long been planned, together with his victorious resurrection: 'He then began to teach them that the Son of Man must suffer many things and be rejected by the elders, the chief priests and the teachers of the law, and that he must be killed and after three days rise again' (Mark 8:31; cf. Mark 10:33–34). And after the resurrection, right at the heart of his teaching was this plan of God, perfectly accomplished in him: ' "Did not the Messiah have to suffer these things and then enter his glory?" And beginning with Moses and all the Prophets, he explained to them what was said in all the Scriptures concerning himself' (Luke 24:26–27).

His disciples too, he said, were part of that plan, and repentance and forgiveness of sins would be preached in his name to all nations:

> He said to them, 'This is what I told you while I was still with you: everything must be fulfilled that is written about me in the Law of Moses, the Prophets and the Psalms.'
>
> Then he opened their minds so they could understand the Scriptures. He told them, 'This is what is written: the Messiah will suffer and rise from the dead on the third day, and repentance for the forgiveness of sins will be preached in his name to all nations, beginning at Jerusalem. You are witnesses of these things.'
> (Luke 24:44–48)

So it was all planned: from Bethlehem to Calvary: 'when the set time had fully come, God sent his Son, born of a woman, born under the law, to redeem those under law, that we might receive adoption to sonship' (Galatians 4:4–5). In the memorable words of one theologian:

> His emergence on earth was as it were the swelling in of heaven. His sacrifice began before He came into the world, and his cross was that of a lamb slain before the world's foundation. There was a Calvary above which was the mother of it all.[4]

The plan of God which includes us

Each and every follower of Christ can know, as he knew, that their earthly life is the outcome of a heavenly plan. As the Lord Jesus saw his life as eternally planned in love and wisdom, so too may we. And those two are inextricably linked: the plan of God for Jesus and the plan of God for us. This is the astonishing and thrilling message of Ephesians 1:

> Praise be to the God and Father of our Lord Jesus Christ, who has blessed us in the heavenly realms with every spiritual blessing in Christ. For he chose us in him before the creation of the world to be holy and blameless in his sight. In love he predestined us for adoption to sonship through Jesus Christ, in accordance with his pleasure and will – to the praise of his glorious grace, which he has freely given us in the One he loves. (Ephesians 1:3–6)

This isn't speculation: it is revelation. What we could never otherwise have known is clearly revealed to us. That revelation arches from eternity past to eternity future, taking in the great plan of God and the end of history, and it does so in a way that does not crush or marginalize us, but in a way that includes and elevates us, and finally identifies us. It is a plan that comes to fulfilment in Jesus Christ and in the transformed lives of all his people: 'For we are God's handiwork, created in Christ Jesus to do good works, which God prepared in advance for us to do' (Ephesians 2:10).

Here we find out who we really are, and the true significance of our existence. For we discover that we were made for our Creator, who has unique and eternal purposes for us, beyond the broken present, beyond the unseen future, beyond the cooling of suns and the death of planets, a future long prepared for, a future with God, and the beginning of a new heaven and a new earth. It staggers the mind and it always will – the plan of God for creation and redemption.

A world beyond worlds

'Praise be to the God and Father of our Lord Jesus Christ, who has blessed us in the heavenly realms with every spiritual blessing in Christ' (Ephesians 1:3). We often feel minute and insignificant as we contemplate the universe, with its unthinkable distances, its immense galaxies and its uncountable stars and planets. But here we are introduced to a higher realm still – the heavenly realms. And here, to our amazement, we are not lost – but found!

By 'the heavenly realms', the apostle Paul does not simply mean a location, but a level of existence in which God has dwelt from all eternity as the Father, the Son and the Holy Spirit, and planned our creation and our eternal salvation. This is a dimension of reality that we as human beings are uniquely meant to know. We are to see our world today in the larger context of that world, and to see our present existence as determined from there. So we are not accidents in time, but purposed people present to the mind of God from all eternity, in the plan of Father, Son and Spirit, and destined to share the eternal life of God.

When we cut ourselves off from all of that, we cut off our chief glory, our true identity, our God-given purpose. We become desperate at the futility of life and death; we become self-centred, driven by greed and lust, by fear and despair. We narrow our horizons until life itself becomes a weariness between the cradle and the grave. Apologist Os Guinness has put it like this:

> Human life has traditionally been lived in a house with windows to other worlds. Those windows may have sometimes become dirty, broken or boarded up, but they were always there. Only in the modern world have we achieved what has been called 'a world without windows'. Shut off from transcendence, modern people are shut up to triviality.[5]

When we read our modern novels and look at our contemporary art, what do we so often find? Men and women crying in the wilderness because of the ultimate futility of life, because of its loneliness and purposelessness and decay. In losing the knowledge of God, we lose the knowledge of ourselves; in losing the knowledge of the 'heavenly realms', of the world beyond worlds, we have no explanation of this universe and no good news of salvation in this fallen and dying world.

In stark contrast, Paul tells us that we, of all people, can be a people of faith and hope and love and praise, because we have heard and received the good news of the gospel: 'Like cold water to a weary soul is good news from a distant land' (Proverbs 25:25). We have access to this knowledge supremely because of Christ. He came from the Father and spoke of that realm; he returned to the Father and will take us to that realm: 'Father, I want those you have given me to be with me where I am, and to see my glory, the glory you have given me because you loved me before the creation of the world' (John 17:24; cf. 8:23–25; 16:28).

Eavesdropping on an eternal conversation

'For he chose us in him before the creation of the world' (Ephesians 1:4).

Here is a plan that was prepared in the counsels of the eternal Godhead, an agreement between the Father, the Son and the Holy Spirit, in full view of the failure of our race and the cost of our redemption. And we learn from this chapter (and others) something which is also astounding: that you and I were mentioned by name in that divine conversation – deliberately, individually, and with full knowledge of our sins and failure.

Jesus spoke repeatedly of those whom God had given him: 'All those the Father gives me will come to me, and whoever comes to me I will never drive away' (John 6:37). They were his sheep, and he had come for them (John 10:27–30). He had given them his Father's word (17:6–12), and his prayer would gather and unite those sheep (17:20–23). To see your life in this context is to solve once and for all the dilemma of who you are, what you are, and why you are given life in this world. God's love may be a new thing in your life, but it is not a new thing in his life. He has loved you with an everlasting love; you have never been lost in the crowd; you have had significance with God from eternity. All this is the foundation of our deep security, peace and joy.

What we were foreordained to be is made explicit in astonishing words: 'In love he predestined us for adoption to sonship through Jesus Christ' (Ephesians 1:5). We are children of God by the adoption of grace through Christ Jesus (Galatians 4:4–7; cf. John 1:12). That is our new identity, and we have the glory of being loved by God. Christlikeness is now the family likeness, which we all bear to some degree, and shall one day do so in full.

All this can be so transforming in our lives as we seek to follow Christ. First, it transforms our view of ourselves: loved with everlasting love by the greatest Persons in the universe – the Father who chose us, the Son who died for us, the Holy Spirit who lives in us. This is surely the greatest antidote to a low self-image, the greatest encouragement when we are confused and disappointed, and the greatest assurance that we shall share the future God has planned for us.

Then it transforms our view of other Christians too. If they mean that much to God, should they not mean much to us also? If we see them as having been named in the divine conversation with infinite love and immeasurable commitment, then we will value them more highly and serve them more cheerfully. Remember, 'whatever you did for one of the least of these brothers and sisters of mine, you did for me' (Matthew 25:40). Our church life and relationships will be profoundly affected if we see the person we tend to neglect, or find difficult, as being a child of God, having been chosen by God and loved before the foundation of the world.

This also gives us strength and confidence in our evangelism, in spite of the indifference or opposition that we so often meet. When the apostle Paul went to Corinth, the risen Christ spoke to him in a vision: 'Do not be afraid; keep on speaking, do not be silent. For I am with you, and no one is going to attack and harm you, because I have many people in this city' (Acts 18:9–10). That statement refers to the plan of God which Paul could not see, but which the risen Lord

could see. The person in your office or family or neighbourhood who seems far from God at present may have been
named in God's plan from the beginning – and you may be
one link in the chain, one step in the progress of the divine
plan for them.

The goal of the plan – Christlikeness

It has been well said that 'for the Christian, heaven is not a
goal; it is a destination. The *goal* is that "Christ be *formed* in
you"' (Galatians 4:19).[6] The goal is Christlikeness.

God has in his mind and on his heart millions of human
beings in all their individuality who will live with him for ever
in the image and likeness of Christ who is the image and
likeness of God:

> And we know that in all things God works for the good of
> those who love him, who have been called according to his
> purpose. For those God foreknew he also predestined to be
> conformed to the image of his Son, that he might be the
> firstborn among many brothers and sisters. And those he
> predestined, he also called; those he called, he also justified;
> those he justified he also glorified.
> (Romans 8:28–30)

What a place heaven and the new earth will be, peopled by
Christlike men and women! This process is begun in the first
moments of the new life when the believer is 'born again',
'born from above', or 'born of God' (John 3:3, 7; 1 John 5:1).
It reaches perfection at the Second Coming of Christ and the
general resurrection. John writes in his letter, 'we know that
when Christ appears, we shall be like him, for we shall see him
as he is' (1 John 3:2b).

Being 'conformed to the image of his Son' (Romans 8:29) is a process that is going on right now as you read this book, or as you pray on the way to work, or as you take your children to school, or as you go to church, or as you witness to Christ, or as you help the needy, or as you pray for them. It is the great work of the Holy Spirit in conjunction with all Jesus has done for us in his earthly life and with all he is praying for us in his heavenly life (John 17:9, 24; Romans 12:2).

Being 'conformed to the image of his Son' speaks of the great and persistent work of the Holy Spirit who partners with the risen Christ: 'And we all, who with unveiled faces contemplate the Lord's glory, are being transformed into his image with ever-increasing glory, which comes from the Lord, who is the Spirit' (2 Corinthians 3:18). This is a work in progress, incomplete, as we all know, but its reality and value are not in doubt: 'For we are God's handiwork ['work of art', Jerusalem Bible], created in Christ Jesus to do good works, which God prepared in advance for us to do' (Ephesians 2:10).

Being 'conformed to the image of his Son' also involves the ways we respond to God in the darker experiences of life: in injustice and loss, in rejection and suffering, in illness and before the approach of death. It involves trusting and worshipping, refusing bitterness and rebellion, 'fixing our eyes on Jesus' (Hebrews 12:2), and recognizing our Father's plan and presence with us, and for us, in it all (Romans 8:28; 2 Corinthians 12:7–10; Hebrews 4:14–16).

When we see each day as a new one in the plan of God for our lives, then that day is touched with a fresh significance. Who is God going to bring to your notice: what conversations, what encounters, what prayers? Ask, 'How can I meet this person, event, opportunity or challenge in the character and likeness of Christ?' When you go out to work or move to a different neighbourhood, or even a different country, recognize that this is part of his plan for your life. When you meet the unexpected twists and turns, and even the disappointments and seeming dead ends of life, then remember that God is at work in it all, lovingly, faithfully, pursuing his plan (Romans 8:28).

2

We have been set apart for God

A story is told of Christopher Columbus's first voyage to the Americas. One of the crew, it is said, was a village cobbler. Seemingly oblivious to the momentous nature of the trip, he spent the whole voyage worrying that his rival in the next village would gain an advantage over him while he was gone.

Amazing really. There he was taking part in one of the greatest events in history, but all he could think of was the local cobbler!

We are all on a journey: the most exciting, far-reaching and potentially glorious one we will ever make. To forget the goal, or to be preoccupied throughout the journey with lesser things, is to lose the chief point. The goal is God – for whom we have been made – a life with God, and a relationship with him that not even death will be allowed to end. When we marginalize God, we marginalize ourselves, for we were made for him, and it is the chief distinction of being human that we can know God and be like him.

There is a clutch of related words in the Bible that all speak of this. Foremost of these is the word 'holiness'. It is a tragedy that in our secular culture this word is so often devalued, and even mocked as weird or irrelevant. John White illustrates this when he asks:

> Have you ever gone fishing in a polluted river and hauled out an old shoe, a tea kettle or a rusty can? I get a similar sort of catch if I cast as a bait the word *holiness* into the murky depths of my mind. To my dismay I come up with such associations as: thinness, hollow-eyed gauntness, beards, sandals, long robes, stone cells, no sex, no jokes, hair shirts, frequent cold baths, fasting, hours of prayer, wild rocky deserts, getting up at 4 A.M., clean fingernails, stained glass, self-humiliation.[1]

Yet such associations are a far cry from the Bible's use of the word 'holiness'. Most of them are irrelevant, some of them are foolish, and all of them are dull. Why? Because they are detached from God who, in his holiness, is the most awesome, the most exciting and the most beautiful Being in the universe, and who calls us to share his holiness as our eternal glory. Dr J. I. Packer summarizes the biblical teaching and its immense privilege in this way:

> Holiness is consecrated closeness to God. Holiness is in essence obeying God, living to God and for God . . . In relation to God, holiness takes the form of a single-minded passion to please by love and loyalty, devotion and praise. In relation to sin, it takes the form of a resistance movement, a discipline of not gratifying the desires of the flesh, but of putting to death the deeds of the body (Rom. 8:13; Gal. 5:16). Holiness is, in a word, God-taught, Spirit-wrought Christlikeness, the sum and substance of committed discipleship, the demonstration of faith working by love, the responsive outflow in righteousness of supernatural life from the hearts of those who are born again.[2]

In the New Testament one of the most important terms for this is 'sanctification', which we met in the preface. It can mean both the *state* of being holy and the *process* of making someone holy. At its root, sanctification is being set apart by God to share his life, and on our side, it is receiving his salvation, bowing to his lordship, adoring his beauty and goodness. It is a takeover bid by God which lifts our small-town, parochial lives into the length and breadth and height and depth of his own life in his Son, Jesus Christ.

We will now focus on a holy God, a holy people, and the application of this for today

1. A holy God

In the Bible, holiness is constantly associated with God. It is so essential to his Being that it is the chief characteristic of all that he is and does. In the Old Testament, for instance, when God comes to people, his first word about himself is: 'I am the LORD . . . and . . . I am holy' (see e.g. Leviticus 11:44; 20:7, 26).

So what does the word mean in its Old Testament context and use? The Hebrew word for 'holy', say scholars, probably comes from a Hebrew root meaning 'cut', that is, 'cut off' from what is ordinary, 'set apart' and 'different'. So the teaching in the Old Testament is that God is cut off, set apart and different. First, he is set apart in his essential and mysterious Being from everything else, from everything finite and created: he is infinite and eternal. And then he is also set apart from everything sinful and corrupt.

The great seventeenth-century Westminster Shorter Catechism asked generations of young people the question: 'What is God?' and responded: 'God is a Spirit, infinite, eternal and unchangeable, in his being, wisdom, power, holiness, justice, goodness and truth', 'a statement which the great Charles Hodge described as "probably the best definition of God ever penned by man"'.[3]

A dangerous holiness!

However, if God is infinitely removed from everything created, he is infinitely removed from everything corrupted also. His majestic holiness involves his ethical holiness: his moral majesty, his utter purity, his white-hot zeal for goodness, righteousness and justice. This made holiness dangerous to fallen human beings, with their sin and corruption, an early lesson in Israel's life in connection with the temple, its rituals and its worship, and its categories of holiness and 'uncleanness'.

But what enabled an approach to God was the blood of atoning sacrifice sprinkled on the altar and poured out at its base. Repeatedly in the Old Testament we are told that sacrifice 'atones' for sin and uncleanness. The meaning involves a number of things, including a ransom, with its idea of a price to be paid, a process of wiping clean, with its idea of removing something entirely, a blotting out, remitting and forgiving sin, and more. But behind it all is a holy and just God whose wrath against corruption and sin is absolute, and whose wrath is turned away from the offerer by means of the sacrifice which is presented as a substitute for the offender. Yet this same holy God is the One who, in love and grace, provides the very means of our protection, and who says of the sacrificial blood, 'I have given it to you to make atonement' (Leviticus 17:11).

The wonderful result is reconciliation with God. Sacrifice enables God, without compromise, to elevate sinful human beings to the level of the 'holy' by cleansing the unclean. 'I the LORD am holy . . . I make you holy' is a repeated refrain in the book of Leviticus, and it is in essence a gospel refrain too (Leviticus 21:8, 15, 23; 22:9, 16, 32). The blood of the atoning sacrifice removes the barrier, enabling God to reconcile us to himself. It is the means of peace and reconciliation: sinners can live at peace with God.

Peace by the blood of Jesus

The New Testament teaches us that this was to prepare us for the one atoning sacrifice which was sufficient for all time and for all people, when the last Priest offered the supreme sacrifice of himself for the sin of the world: 'by one sacrifice he has made perfect for ever those who are being made holy' (Hebrews 10:14). This was no mere earthly priest, but 'the Lamb of God, who takes away the sin of the world!': Jesus, who makes us holy by his blood (John 1:29; Hebrews 10:11–14).

The apostle Paul expresses it in legal categories. It took all the resources of the Godhead to deal with the problem of sin and reconcile to himself the ungodly, the rebellious and the condemned. This was the problem: how to justify sinners and still remain just; how to put away sin without cover-up; how to satisfy both his love and his justice.

Sooner than compromise any part of his holiness, God himself would satisfy all its demands:

> God presented Christ as a sacrifice of atonement, through the shedding of his blood – to be received by faith. He did this to demonstrate his righteousness . . . at the present time, so as to be just and the one who justifies those who have faith in Jesus. (Romans 3:25–26)

The cross was God's tsunami where the whole tidal wave of divine wrath for human rebellion and sin, its long history of cruelty and pride, engulfed the Son of God. Here Jesus Christ became the representative of sinners before the bar of God's justice; he took personal responsibility for our sins. He stood in our place on earth so that we might stand in his place in heaven.

He suffered under God's curse not for his own sins, but for ours: 'Christ redeemed us from the curse of the law by becoming a curse for us' (Galatians 3:13); 'God made him who had no sin to be sin for us, so that in him we might become the righteousness of God' (2 Corinthians 5:21).

'The cross was simultaneously an act of punishment and amnesty, severity and grace, justice and mercy.'[4] The Judge was judged in our place that we might go free in the justification that comes from God, 'ransomed, healed, restored, forgiven'.[5] On this basis we can become God's holy people, and God's plan for his people in all ages can be put into effect (John 17:18–19).

2. A holy people

We tend to think of holiness as coming only at the end of a long and often painful process. But in the Old and the New Testaments, we learn the important lesson that holiness is given *to* us before it is demanded *of* us. We are *made* holy before we are commanded to *be* holy. So holiness is not, in the first place, something you or I do – it's something done to us. As the word suggests, we have been 'set apart' as the special possession of God. This is not a description of our own moral state in the first place, but of our relationship with God, which he has established on the basis of his Son's finished work (Romans 5:9–11).

This lesson is repeatedly taught to the Old Testament people of God. In the book of Exodus we read that God chose to make Israel a holy nation. In a great event at the foot of Mount Sinai, with Moses as his intermediary, God set them apart publicly and formally for himself, making them 'holy', dedicated to God and different from every other nation, and he did so there and then. And so we read repeatedly, 'I am the LORD, who makes you holy' (see Exodus 31:13; Leviticus 20:8; 21:8).

The point is that Israel was made holy by an *act* of God before she lived out her holy standing with God as a *process*. Her standing before God as a holy nation was the starting point, and she was to live out of that truth and live up to it. Israel was to be consistently what God had made her definitively (see Deuteronomy 7:6; 26:16–19).

Saints alive!

We find the same truth in the New Testament in connection with the people of God as individuals. There is a word, a title in fact, which is repeatedly used of all Christian believers, one which today is commonly misused and misunderstood: the word 'saint'. The NIV renders this as 'God's holy people', but other translations use the word 'saint'.

The apostle Paul writes, 'To the saints who are in Ephesus, and are faithful in Christ Jesus' (Ephesians 1:1, ESV), and 'To all the saints in Christ Jesus who are at Philippi' (Philippians 1:1, ESV) and 'To all those in Rome who are loved by God and called to be saints' (Romans 1:7, ESV; that is, not called to become saints, but effectively called with the result that they are indeed saints). He writes to the Corinthians using a related word (which we met earlier): 'To . . . those *sanctified* [set apart] in Christ Jesus and called to be holy people, together with all those everywhere who call on the name of our Lord Jesus Christ – their Lord and ours' (1 Corinthians 1:2, italics mine).

A schoolteacher asked her class for the definition of a saint. Eager young hands went up. One boy suggested, 'A saint is a dead clergyman, sir', and one girl said, 'A saint is someone the light shines through', thinking perhaps of a stained-glass window and its figures (not a bad definition, maybe, in another context!). In fact, the word 'saint' means 'set-apart one', and a saint is anyone (and everyone) who has been effectively called by God to become his special possession, his son or daughter in Christ Jesus (John 1:12).

Sainthood then is not the finishing point of the Christian life, but the starting point, the root and impetus of all 'saintliness' that follows. As Dr J. I. Packer puts it, 'The New Testament does not say that Christians must lead holy lives in order to become saints; instead it tells Christians that because they are saints they must lead holy lives.'[6]

The apostle Peter sums up much of what has been said earlier, using terms constantly found in the Old Testament to describe Israel, and employing them to describe all believers, Jew and Gentile, who belong to the Israel of God:

> But you are a chosen people, a royal priesthood, a holy nation, God's special possession, that you may declare the praises of him who called you out of darkness into his wonderful light. Once you were not a people, but now you are the people of God; once you had not received mercy, but now you have received mercy.
> (1 Peter 2:9–10)

3. The call to holiness

With privilege comes obligation, as we know, and with the privilege of belonging to God comes the obligation to walk in his ways, to love and serve him, and to love and serve others as he loves and serves both us and them. At the start of her life as a nation, Israel is reminded that her new identity involves duty as well as privilege, and this extends to the external life and daily relationships of all her people.

Living as the people of God

In his classic book on Old Testament ethics, *Living as the People of God*, Christopher Wright comments on God's words to the nation in Leviticus 19:2, 'Be holy because I, the LORD your God, am holy':

> We are inclined to think of 'holiness' as a matter of personal piety . . . But the rest of Leviticus 19 shows us that the kind of holiness which reflects God's own holiness is thoroughly practical. It includes generosity to the poor at harvest time, justice for workers, integrity in judicial processes, considerate behaviour to other people, equality before the law for immigrants, honest trading and other very 'earthy' social matters. And all through the chapters runs the refrain: 'I am the LORD', as if to say, 'This is what I require of you because this is what I myself would do.'

In Deuteronomy 10 and elsewhere in the Old Testament holiness is described as 'walking in God's ways'. So what are God's ways? Chris Wright points out:

> The answer is given first in broad terms. His was a way of condescending love in choosing Abraham and his descendants to be the special vehicle of his blessing . . . That required an inward response of love and humility in return . . . But what specifically were the 'ways' of God, in which Israel was to walk? This passage singles out a few:

'He shows no partiality and accepts no bribes. He defends
the cause of the fatherless and the widow, and loves the
alien, giving him food and clothing. And you are to love
those who are aliens, for you yourselves were aliens in
Egypt' (Deuteronomy 10:17–19).[7]

In the book of Proverbs too, what it means to walk with God
emerges in the way that so many of the little details of
behaviour commended in the book do indeed reflect the
character of God himself. There is emphasis on the virtues
of faithfulness, kindness, work, compassion, social justice,
especially for the poor and oppressed, generosity, impartiality
and incorruptibility. All this brings us down to earth with a
bang! Or should we say with an 'Amen'? It means we cannot
reduce such a massive thing as being set apart for God to a
devout daydream. But it also means we can glorify God in our
daily and down-to-earth lives. As the apostle Peter says:

> Therefore, with minds that are alert and fully sober, set your
> hope on the grace to be brought to you when Jesus Christ is
> revealed at his coming. As obedient children, do not conform
> to the evil desires you had when you lived in ignorance. But
> just as he who called you is holy, so be holy in all you do;
> for it is written: 'Be holy, because I am holy.'
> (1 Peter 1:13–16)

Holiness is a gift, but it is also a calling. Holiness is a lifelong
programme: growing in grace and in the image of the Lord
Jesus Christ (Ephesians 4:22 – 5:20; Colossians 3:1–17). We
may be rightly secure in our faith, but we must also be
energized, challenged and directed by it. Our calling is not to
rely and relax, but to trust and obey. As Jim Packer says,
'Holiness is no more by faith without effort than it is by effort

without faith.'[8] We are called to live in the relationship God has established with us, and out of the identity he has given us in Christ, a life that can sing as it struggles and as it follows Christ in faith wherever he leads.

Drinking and singing God!

Eugene Peterson got it right:

> The God-life cannot be domesticated or used – it can only be entered into on its own terms. Holiness does not make God smaller so that he can be used in convenient and manageable projects; it makes us larger so that God can give out life through us, extravagantly, spontaneously. The holy is an interior fire, a passion for living in and for God, a capacity for exuberance in the presence of God. There are springs deep within and around us from which we can drink and sing God.[9]

Are we, as set-apart Christians, 'drinking and singing God' today and every day?

This leads us into another foundational area of Christlikeness: union with Christ.

3

We are united to Christ for ever

Rory Shiner, a minister with responsibility for two university-based congregations in Perth, Australia, has written a sparkling book on union with Christ entitled *One Forever* which explores the meaning and implications of this term. In an earlier article he had pointed out that the Bible's favourite way of describing our relationship with Jesus Christ is one that we hardly ever use. 'The idea of union with Christ', he says, 'has not invaded our language, our prayers, our songs and our imaginations in the way (for example) the husband-wife or friend-friend relationship has.' 'Why is that?' he asks.

He admits that most of us find such biblical terms as 'in Christ' rather difficult and even obscure:

I mean, what does it mean exactly to be *in* Christ, or for that matter, in anyone? If someone tells me I *follow* Christ, I get that. *Under* Christ? Yes, I know what it means to be under someone. *Saved* by Christ? Got it. *Inspired* by? Check. And so on. They are concepts I understand: Christ as a leader, a lord, a saviour. But '*in* Christ' almost seems to portray Christ as a place, a sphere, a location. How does that work?

He then gives us an illustration of what it means:

> Imagine yourself at the airport, about to board a plane. The plane is on its way to sunny Melbourne, and Melbourne is where you want to be. What relationship do you need to have with the plane at this point?
>
> Would it help to be *under* the plane, to *submit* yourself to the plane's eminent authority in the whole flying-to-Melbourne thing? Or would it help to be *inspired* by the plane? To watch it fly off and whisper, 'One day, I hope to do that too'. What about *following* the plane? You know the plane is going to Melbourne, and so it stands to reason that if you take note of the direction it goes and pursue it then you too will end up there.
>
> Of course, the key relationship you need with the plane is not to be under it, behind it, or inspired by it. You need to be *in* it. Why? Because, by being in the plane, what happens to the plane will also happen to you. The question 'Did you get to Melbourne?' will be part of a larger question: 'Did the plane get to Melbourne?' If the answer to the second question is yes, and if you were in the plane, then what happened to the plane will also have happened to you.

Shiner comments further:

> I think, at heart, the biblical idea of being in Christ is something like that. According to the New Testament, to be in Christ is to say that, by union with him, whatever is true of him is now true of us. He died, we died. He is raised, we are (and will be) raised . . . He is loved, we are loved. And so on, all because we are in him.[1]

We may be anxious like first-time travellers, or confident like seasoned ones, and we may spend the journey working or

worrying, preparing for arrival or fretting about the things
we left unfinished at home. But the plane is bigger than
us and our fears, and it will get us there – in one shape or
another!

Of course, the illustration has its limits, and no one would
think we were being asked to lie back in our everyday lives
and let Jesus do it all without us. There is a whole pilgrim's
progress of challenge and effort, as well as security and confidence, involved in the Christian life. But behind us and
around us and before us, in all our experiences, victories
and defeats, is the reality of our being 'in Christ'.

Ultimately, there is no explanation or analogy that is sufficient; this mystery of Christ's union with the believer is 'by
its nature incomprehensible'.[2] 'It is in some way a union of
two spirits which does not extinguish either of them.'[3] It is
helpfully illustrated in several ways in the New Testament, for
example, by the union of husband and wife in marriage
(Ephesians 5:32), by the union between vine and branches
(John 15:1–7) and by the union of stones in the building of a
temple (Ephesians 2:20–22).

Dr Robert Letham has written a profound and valuable
book on this. He says in its introduction, 'Union with Christ
is right at the centre of the Christian doctrine of salvation.
The whole of our relationship with God can be summed up
in such terms.' Our *justification* before God is 'grounded on
union with Christ'. It is 'the foundational basis for *sanctification* and the dynamic force that empowers it', and 'the
resurrection of believers at the Return of Christ is a resurrection *in Christ*'.[4]

In the Gospels Jesus gives us two powerful illustrations of
this union. The first is baptism, which teaches it in dramatic
form, and the second is the vine and its branches, as mentioned
above.

1. Baptized into Christ

> Then Jesus came to them and said, 'All authority in heaven
> and on earth has been given to me. Therefore go and make
> disciples of all nations, baptising them in the name of the
> Father and of the Son and of the Holy Spirit, and teaching
> them to obey everything I have commanded you. And surely
> I am with you always, to the very end of the age.'
> (Matthew 28:18–20)

I've baptized hundreds of new Christians with the famous
baptismal formula at the end of Matthew's Gospel: 'My
brother/my sister, on the confession of your faith I now
baptize you into the name of the Father and of the Son and
of the Holy Spirit.' But as you might have noticed, there is
one word which has been changed. Most translations say, '*in*
the name of the Father and of the Son and of the Holy Spirit';
I change 'in' to 'into', which is often the marginal reading. I
do so first of all because that is a perfectly reasonable trans-
lation of the original Greek word, which means both 'in' and
'into', but second, because it emphasizes what is symbolically
happening here (Romans 6:3).

The person has not only been drawn to God, but also
drawn into the life of God, the life he has for his people in an
eternal relationship with them, drawn into the life of the
Father, the Son and the Holy Spirit. This is usually focused
on Christ, because he is the 'way into' this life, God having
reconciled us to himself by the atoning death of his Son (Acts
2:38; 10:48; Galatians 3:27).

We have the stunning privilege in Christ of belonging to
the fellowship of the Holy Trinity. Just think of it! You can say,
'I belong to God; I am part of the life and fellowship of God,
Father, Son and Spirit; they live in conscious fellowship with

one another *and with me (!)*, and share with me their life of love, of joy and of promise.'

This is a new kind of life, but it has been preceded by a kind of death. In fact, the service of baptism has been described as a funeral service with a built-in resurrection! It depicts in vivid form Christ's own death, burial and resurrection for us, and our part in it depicts our personal union with him in all he has done for us and our acceptance of the new life he offers to all who come to him. We proclaim that we have become sharers in his atoning death and victorious resurrection. We were 'buried with him in baptism' and 'raised with him' (Colossians 2:12; cf. Romans 6:4; Galatians 2:20).

New Lord, new life, new lifestyle

At the believer's baptism there is a baptismal death. In Paul's terms, we have 'died to the law through the body of Christ' (Romans 7:4). Here he sees us as prisoners who have died to the condemnation of the law of God because of our sin; we are as out of reach to the punishments of the law as a dead man might be. But we have died to the law that we 'might belong to another, to him who was raised from the dead, in order that we might bear fruit for God'. There has been a death to old loyalties, old obligations, old enmities, and above all an old identity. There is a rising to new life with a new ownership and a new identity. We are no longer rebels, but children; God is no longer the enemy, but the Father.

Paul expressed it very dramatically when he wrote to the Galatians, 'I have been crucified with Christ and I no longer live, but Christ lives in me. The life I now live in the body, I live by faith in the Son of God, who loved me and gave himself for me' (Galatians 2:20). These are not merely ethical categories, but they do have all kinds of ethical implications and outworkings.

When a person becomes a man or woman 'in Christ', the past and the present meet. Christ's history becomes their history; his past achievement becomes the foundation of their present justification; his right becomes their claim. But in addition to that, what was done *for* them becomes operative *in* them, the impetus of their actions and the motivation behind their decisions. A historic creed becomes a daily reality: 'In the same way, count yourselves dead to sin but alive to God in Christ Jesus' (Romans 6:11; see also 13:14).

This being 'alive to God' is a vital reality in our union with Christ by the Holy Spirit. We saw earlier that we are described as 'God's handiwork', 'God's work of art', 'created in Christ Jesus to do good works, which God prepared in advance for us to do' (Ephesians 2:10). This new life in Christ 'describes an entirely new kind of life – a life filled with good works, sparkling with love and devoted to God's glory'.[5]

The corporate Christ

Being 'in Christ' is, however, a concept larger and wider than either the individual's status or experience. Hence, Paul writes 'To all God's people in Christ Jesus at Philippi' and speaks of 'God's churches in Judea, which are in Christ Jesus' (Philippians 1:1; 1 Thessalonians 2:14). It involves the whole church, for the universal church is in him (Ephesians 1:22–23; 5:32). 'In him' everything finds its beginning and its end (Colossians 1:15–20).

He is the last Adam, and in him there is a renewed humanity: 'For as in Adam all die, so in Christ all will be made alive' (1 Corinthians 15:22; cf. Romans 5:12–19). All the people *of* Christ Jesus are people *in* Christ Jesus, individually and corporately considered: millions of us, the whole church of Christ, past, present and future. There are few more profound testimonies to the divinity of Christ.

2. Growing in Christ: the vine and the branches

In order to teach the idea of union with him as the secret of the Christian's ongoing life and spiritual growth, Jesus used another object lesson, in the illustration of the vine and the branches: 'I am the true vine, and my Father is the gardener'; 'I am the vine; you are the branches' (John 15:1, 5).

This union is not merely nominal or formal, but vital. The life of the vine flows to the branches, and the branches bear fruit as a result. The life of the risen glorified Christ is achieved in us by the Holy Spirit, who is the connecting link and channel between the Saviour in heaven and the believer on earth.

This fruit is not rare or unlikely, or beyond the power of ordinary Christians; it is in fact natural to the new nature that we have received from Christ. A popular television gardener likes to say of growing young plants, 'It's not difficult; it's not complicated. You can do it; *they want to grow.*' So I might say similarly, there is a new life within each of us that wants to grow, and the fruit of the Spirit will grow if we remain in Christ.

The result of this is fruitfulness: 'If you remain in me and I in you, you will bear much fruit' (John 15:5). But that promise comes with a warning. 'Remain in me, as I also remain in you. No branch can bear fruit by itself; it must remain in the vine. Neither can you bear fruit unless you remain in me' (verse 4).

There are many forces in this world that would detach you from Christ, reducing your vital Christianity to formal church attendance perhaps, or filling your horizon with personal ambition and material gain, or captivating your heart with a forbidden love, an attraction, even a seduction, that drains the spiritual life in you.

How can you remain close to Christ? How can you do your part? It involves continuing to be open to his influence and his Word: read your Bible; pray every day; seek ways to love and serve others in the church and in the world around you; cultivate the fruit of the Spirit which is the result of his indwelling: 'love, joy, peace, forbearance, kindness, goodness, faithfulness, gentleness and self-control' (Galatians 5:22–23), and much more. These are the most valuable things in life, and they enrich a person as wealth and prestige can never do.

Pruning the vines

However, our growth and fruitfulness is not done in a hurry, or without care and the disciplines of life with God. So Jesus speaks here too of those disciplines using the metaphor of pruning: 'I am the true vine, and my Father is the gardener. He cuts off every branch in me that bears no fruit, while every branch that does bear fruit he prunes so that it will be even more fruitful' (John 15:1–2).

It's staggering how much pruning a vine can take, and God uses all kinds of life events to prune each one of us, young and old, strong and weak, and he does so with one aim: that we might grow in grace and godliness.

I have known weak believers become strong because something came into their lives that brought a painful halt to their plans and expectations. They sought God and found him in an experience which reordered their priorities. His pruning turned a weak plant into a strong one. Many have seen a sincere faith become a stronger one by the shock of some dramatic loss or disappointment, or even by being brought close to death through accident or illness. I think of a young pharmacist in our church from a Christian family, nearly killed in a car accident outside his hospital, who determined to give two years of his life to a pharmacy in Africa because his experiences had provoked new growth in him.

I have known strong believers who were already fruitful for God demonstrate great patience and perseverance in the face of setbacks and new challenges. Even a strong plant needs to be pruned, and many a believer might have grown complacent, their fruitfulness diminishing, if they had not been cut back for a while. I think of a young teacher, discovering that she had diabetes, saying to me, 'I do not believe God wants to heal me of this condition but to use it for his glory. And I want to do that too, beginning in the staffroom at school where they are all deeply concerned and wondering how I can square this with my assurance that God loves me.'

Then see how personal it suddenly becomes as Jesus continues. Vines can teach lessons, but only 'persons' can love.

Christlikeness – the family likeness

'As the Father has loved me, so have I loved you. Now remain in my love . . . My command is this: love each other as I have loved you' (John 15:9, 12).

So the Lord Jesus speaks of the love of the Father for the Son, and the love of the Son for his people, and in the shared love of God little people like you and me can find a great destiny: 'As the Father has loved me, so have I loved you. Now remain in my love' (verse 9).

Furthermore, if we are 'in Christ', then we are *together* in him. In all our diversities of age and gifts, of gender and personality, of experience and achievement, we all share one life as the family of God, with one family likeness, the most significant and outstanding characteristic of which is love.

So the new communities that Jesus is bringing into being are to be communities of love (1 John 4:7–12) in a world all too short of love. Love is to be their firstfruit, after which the other fruit will follow. It is to be a love that is modelled on Jesus' supreme self-giving ('as I have loved you', John 15:12), a love sustained by his Spirit bringing his life into our hearts. Their heartbeat is to be the same. There will be a new instinct in them, and a new power given to them to put it into action.

Bearing fruit in Christ

'If you remain in me and I in you, you will bear much fruit' (John 15:5). Here is great encouragement for all of us. It is not a matter of dramatic opportunities or exotic experiences or great achievements, but a matter of 'remaining' in him: humble, reliant, loving, willing.

Fruit will differ in different lives and at different times. Some will bear fruit in sickness and bereavement, others in their working lives and vocations, others as evangelists, pastors and teachers. Sometimes the fruit will only appear long after an event, as it did with the young woman on the London bus.

The young woman on the London bus

Let me explain. For many years our church has been largely composed of young families and students, but last year we held our first 'Grandparents' Morning'. Thirty or forty of us spent time sharing with, and praying for, one another, remembering the challenges and opportunities, as well as the privileges, of being grandparents. Two who came were from another church, and they told me the following remarkable story about themselves.

Eighteen-year-old Trish Oxley was standing in a crowded bus crossing Waterloo Bridge in March 1964. A passenger sitting nearby was reading a copy of the *News of the World*, and an article caught her eye. It concerned a young man who had been put out of his home, disowned by his family and seriously harassed by the leaders of the local Exclusive Brethren assembly to which he had belonged but which he now wanted to leave. Trish felt the Lord was telling her to pray for this man. She told me, 'Over the following months I prayed faithfully that God would be with this young man and take care of him.'

Some years later she got married and forgot about the episode. Her young husband, Alex Slater, worked for the Fishermen's Mission. Then, one day, when they were living in Shetland with their two children, a book arrived for Alex. It was inscribed thus: 'With memories of the past, see page 80'. The sender was the journalist who had written the original story in the *News of the World*, the writer Norman Adams. As she read, Trish suddenly remembered the article she had seen on the London bus and realized that *the young man she had prayed for over eight years earlier was the man she had been married to for four years!* 'Yes,' she said later, 'God did take care of him, but I never expected that God would use me as the answer to that prayer.'

For four years Trish Slater had lived with the fruit of her prayers without knowing it, but it was there nonetheless. 'If you remain in me and I in you, you will bear much fruit' (John 15:5).

There is a life of adventure before us when we are 'in Christ'. He often takes us in unexpected directions and to unexpected people and tasks. But there is always the Lord's 'well done' that hovers over it even before the last word is spoken over our lives (Matthew 25:21, 23; Hebrews 6:10). I love to render Paul's words in Colossians 3:3 as, 'your life is now *wrapped up* with Christ in God'!

These first chapters have dealt with great foundational truths. In the next section we shall see their practical out-working in the Christian life, deepening and developing the life of Christ in us day by day as we fix our eyes on Jesus and open our lives to his Word and Spirit.

Part 2
The model of Christlikeness

4

The down-to-earth God

A voyeur culture?

In recent years reality TV has been hugely popular: programmes like *Big Brother* and *I'm a Celebrity . . . Get Me Out of
Here!* can become compulsive viewing. In this connection, one
Christian leader made the perceptive comment that we have
become a 'voyeur culture', with many of us preferring to
watch rather than take part.

When I first read that comment, my reaction was to agree,
but with some complacency, because I have always found such
programmes to be mind-numbingly boring.

Then I reminded myself that I like watching gardening
programmes on TV, but do very little gardening myself –
preferring to watch others instead. I even occasionally watch
programmes where people build houses, or decorate or
redesign rooms, although I'd be bored stiff doing it myself and
would make a terrible job of it anyway. But seeing someone
sawing away merrily, or laying bricks swiftly and accurately,
or painting ceilings and walls, is really rather satisfying . . . in

an abstract and uninvolved sort of way. So maybe I too am part of the voyeur culture after all?

But what of God? Is he too the God who watches from the sidelines, silent, uninvolved, immune? Or is he the God who passionately upholds creation and the world we spoiled, the God who gives us our gifts, and speaks in our consciences, and keeps our civilizations and families going; the God who supports the weak, comforts the bereaved, bears with the wayward, the careless and the selfish, and holds back his wrath from the wicked lest the whole world of fallen humanity be consumed in the chain reaction. That certainly sounds more like the God of the Psalms.

The down-to earth-God

We have seen in Part 1 of this book that the God of the New Testament gospel is found anywhere but on the sidelines. He is found in a manger in crowded Bethlehem, in the flight to Egypt from Herod's hatred, and among the refugees of the world, his parents fleeing tyranny and death. Later he is found in a carpenter's shop in an obscure village in the hills of Galilee, living the very ordinary life of a humble worker. Later still he is found nailed to a cross in a sea of agony, crying out in the darkness, and finally he is found dead and delivered to friends for burial. Not much immunity there.

Yet while God is not part of the voyeur culture, we often like to think he is. We stuff our fingers in our ears and complain that he is silent even when he is shouting in our consciences and speaking to us all in the testimony of a million Bibles and in churches on every street corner. We shut our eyes tightly – and then complain of the dark! We ask, 'Why doesn't God do something? – but without interfering with us and our freedoms and choices and lifestyles and comforts, please.

As Christians, we are not allowed simply to care about suffering and despair in our world, but we are challenged to *do* something about it. As the great French novelist Honoré de Balzac once put it, 'It is easy to sit up and take notice. What is difficult is getting up and taking action.' We have our model of engagement in the Son of God, who 'though he was rich, yet for your sake he became poor, so that you through his poverty might become rich' (2 Corinthians 8:9). The Son of God entered one kind of poverty that he might save us from all kinds of poverty, and the gospel is all about sharing the riches of his risen, glorious existence, riches so dearly bought and so freely offered.

An involved Jesus

In a celebrated passage the apostle Paul directs the attention of the Philippian Christians to the incarnation of Christ as a counter to selfishness and vanity, and a spur to self-giving love:

> In your relationships with one another, have the same
> mindset as Christ Jesus:
>
> who, being in very nature God,
> > did not consider equality with God something
> > > to be used to his own advantage;
> rather, he made himself nothing
> > by taking the very nature of a servant,
> > being made in human likeness.
> (Philippians 2:5–7)

This passage doesn't simply tell us that Christ had equality with God – it tells us what he did with it. He did not consider this equality something to be used for *his own* advantage, but instead considered it something to be used for *our* advantage. He did not use his position to keep himself out of trouble, but to help us in our trouble. Indeed, he regarded his equality with God not as excusing him from the task of redemptive suffering, but as uniquely qualifying him for that task.

All power was his, yet he used his power to assume our weakness, his perfect blessedness and freedom from all ill to share our vulnerability and poverty, our dying lives and our painful deaths. He used all that power not to become strong, but to become weak!

It was just like God. Father, Son and Holy Spirit conspired together with the whole resources of the Godhead to produce a pinpoint foetus in a virgin's womb, a baby lying in a manger, one who would be Immanuel, God with us, God one with us, God one of us. The Father sent him, the Spirit prepared him a body and a full human nature, and the Son took that humanity up into his own being, becoming both God and man.

The extent of Christ's involvement

The degree to which the Son of God 'used' his privileges is continued in Paul's vivid statement: 'he made himself nothing by taking the very nature of a servant, being made in human likeness' (verse 7).

The eternal second person of the Trinity began to live his life on two levels, through two natures, living simultaneously the massive life of the Godhead and the creaturely and painful life of our humanity: one person in two natures.

When we say Jesus Christ is 100% God and 100% man, that means we must be as thorough in what we say about his humanity as in what we say about his deity. We cannot exaggerate the degree to which he was human. He was all that we are, except for sin.

He took upon himself, and lived through, a full human nature: not only a human body, not only a human physiology, but a human psychology too. The God who knew all things also knew what it was not to know; the God who was all-powerful also knew what it was to be weak and helpless; the Ancient of Days knew what it was like to grow up as a normal child, increasing in knowledge and understanding and maturity.

So he did not only come *among* us, but he *became* one of us. He lived in and through a true and fully human nature. In that humanity he felt pleasure and pain just as we feel them. He laughed and cried, hoped and feared, and knew delight and disappointment. The Son of God came into our world not as Superman, but as everyman, not as a Hollywood Jesus, but as a next-door Jesus.

What a rebuke this is to our pride, selfishness and self-love. We seek privileges; he surrendered them. We exploit them to our best advantage; he invested them in the needs of others. 'He made himself nothing.' In the words of Augustine, 'The only remedy for the pride of man was the humility of God.'[1]

The depth of Christ's involvement

There is also humiliation. We can see the depths of this in his obedience to death, 'even death on a cross', where 'God made him who had no sin to be sin for us, so that in him we might become the righteousness of God' (2 Corinthians 5:21). That humiliation is foreshadowed when we see the Son of God standing in the waters of John the Baptist's baptism of repentance for the forgiveness of sins. What is the Son of God doing there of all places?

I have always found a story by John White to be a profound illustration of this. He writes:

As a medical student I once missed a practical class on venereal disease. Because of this I had to go to the venereal diseases clinic alone one night, at a time when students did not usually attend. As I entered the building a male nurse I did not know met me. A line of men were waiting for treatment.

'I want to see the doctor,' I said.

'That's what everybody wants. Stand in the line,' he replied.

'But you don't understand. I'm a medical student,' I protested.

'Makes no difference. You got it the same way everybody else did. Stand in the line,' the male nurse repeated.

In the end I managed to explain to him why I was there, but I can still feel the sense of shame that made me balk at standing in the line with men who had VD. Yet Jesus shunned shame as he stood alongside sinners. And the moral gulf that separated him from us was far greater than that separating me from the men at the clinic. Moreover my dislike of venereal disease was as nothing compared with Jesus' utter abhorrence of sin. But he crossed the gulf, joined our ranks, embraced us and still remained pure.[2]

This is what it meant for our Lord to take the very nature of a servant. His sign henceforth would not be a symbol of power, but of loving, self-giving servanthood; not the sword or the warhorse, but the towel and the washbasin and the cross. He who fashioned galaxies would wash feet; he who called angels 'servants' would call us 'friends': the Son of Man 'did not come to be served, but to serve, and to give his life as a ransom for many' (Mark 10:45).

The incarnation of God was no romance, but, as we saw earlier, a stern and costly reality. He fulfilled the will of God in a fallen world: our own all-too-familiar world of competing self-interest and ruthless power play, of unbelief and ingratitude, of toil and sickness. Finally, his Father would take him to a cross where anyone could see a tortured body, but only God could know the full extent of his suffering when he made his soul 'an offering for sin' and 'bore our sins in his body on the cross' (see Isaiah 53:10; 1 Peter 2:24).

As Harry Blamires put it:

> A God who knows exactly what it is to eat a meal and to take a walk, to have a tooth-ache and a stomach-ache, to rejoice at a wedding and to mourn at a funeral, to be indebted to an earthly mother and her husband, to stand trial in a human court, to be flogged, to be cruelly executed, does not need to apologise to men and women for his immunity, still less for his existence.[3]

A call for our involvement

We might see this whole Bible passage as a call to the imitation of Christ. But mere imitation, of course, is not enough: the believer's union with Christ (as we saw earlier) is such that the Christian has the desire to live out the life he has put within us, a desire to follow him born out of worship and love and like-mindedness. One theologian of an earlier generation preached a sermon, 'Imitating the Incarnation', in which he says, 'Next to our longing to be *in* Christ is our corresponding longing to be *like* Christ.'[4] In the same vein, the great Augustine wrote memorably, 'You would perhaps be ashamed to imitate a lowly man; then at least imitate a lowly God.'[5]

If we are to imitate Christ in his incarnation, we must learn that we hold our privileges for others: not for our immunity, but for their assistance. This is especially true among church members: no real need should continue to be unmet among the family of believers. But it is a principle that goes far beyond churches and their life: 'Therefore, as we have opportunity, let us do good to all people, especially to those who belong to the family of believers' (Galatians 6:10).

Most of us have a considerable amount of capital in our congregations: wealth and talent, youth and strength, time and opportunity. And above all, we have the saving knowledge of the true God. We can use our advantages either for immunity or for involvement. Jesus' momentous act of incarnation calls us to see our privileges as opportunities for service.

And it is in the world of the school and the hospital, the world of stressed-out people in the office and heartbroken people in collapsing marriages, the world of the prison and the refugee camp, that Christians are called to live with the mindset of the incarnate Son of God.

Only as we rediscover and lay hold of the real God, the true gospel, the living Christ who came down to earth, will our faith and spirituality make a difference in this world to which he came and in which he works today through those who are willing to imitate the incarnation (1 Corinthians 11:1; 1 Thessalonians 1:6; 2:14; Hebrews 6:11–12; 13:7–8). This will mean getting involved in needs and heartaches, sicknesses and failures, poverty and helplessness. We will use our resources, our privileges and our strength to help others, to lift them up, get alongside them and love them. The greatest need of the world today is for a church that will imitate Christ's incarnation.

John Stott at Keswick

The late John Stott had some challenging words for us all in his last sermon at the Keswick Convention:

In John 20:21, in prayer, Jesus said, 'As you, Father, have sent me into the world, so I send them into the world' – that is us. And in his commissioning in John 17 he says, 'As the Father sent me into the world, so I send you.' These words are immensely significant. This is not just the Johannine version of the Great Commission, but it is also an instruction that their mission in the world was to resemble Christ's mission. In what respect? The key words in these texts are 'sent into the world'. As Christ had entered our world, so we are to enter other people's worlds. It was eloquently explained by Archbishop Michael Ramsey some years ago: 'We state and commend the faith only in so far as we go out and put ourselves with loving sympathy inside the doubts of the doubters, the questions of the questioners and the loneliness of those who have lost the way.'

This entering into other people's worlds is exactly what we mean by incarnational evangelism. All authentic mission is incarnational mission. We are to be like Christ in his mission.[6]

God is the God of incarnation, of life on earth, of daily life and daily encounters: the God of mangers and maternity wards, carpenters' shops and courses for joinery, and schools and hospitals. If we follow him, he will lead us not so much to idyllic retreats, but more often to busy offices and crowded streets, and to everyday events and ordinary people.

As Eugene Peterson expressed it in a book on Christian spirituality:

The Christian life is in perpetual danger of dissolving into wonderful ideas or sublime feelings or ambitious projects . . . This Gospel continues, century after century, generation after generation, as one of our very best defences against a spirituality that is abstracted from the actual lives in which we follow Jesus, one step at a time, walking from kitchen to bedroom, from parking lot to workplace, from sanctuary to cemetery, from classroom to playing field, slugging it out with 'the things in the world . . . the lust of the flesh and the lust of the eyes and the pride of life . . .' (1 John 2:15–16 RSV).[7]

It has been said that we all believe in the God of the heroic, but what we need most days is the God of the humdrum, the commonplace, the everyday. Some of us shrink from the heroic, but every day we will pass by opportunities that even the most timid and least adventurous person can meet.

What is the name of the cleaner?

During her second month of nursing school, the professor gave the students a quiz. The last question stumped most people in the class. It read, 'What is the first name of the woman who cleans the school?'

All the students had seen the cleaning woman several times. She was tall, dark-haired and in her fifties, but how would any of them know her name? Before class ended, one student asked if the last question would count toward their grade.

'Absolutely,' said the professor. 'In your careers you will meet many people. All are significant. They deserve your attention and care, even if all you do is smile and say hello.'

The students have never forgotten that lesson. They also learned her name was Dorothy.[8]

While the great act of incarnation has within itself all the implications and suggestion of self-giving love and service, it is in our Lord's teaching, famously and vividly expressed in the Sermon on the Mount, that the challenge of Christlikeness is most directly presented to us, and to that we now turn.

5

This is your life: the Sermon on the Mount

A pampered pilgrim's progress

I was reading a *Saga* advertisement a while back. (Well, when you get to my age, you do things like that.) It was about following the route of the Pilgrim's Way in Spain to the famous cathedral of Santiago de Compostela, a pilgrimage tradition that began about 1,200 years ago, and all because someone thought they had discovered the remains of St James the apostle.

Pilgrims began flocking to the site on foot, on horseback, and even on their knees as a penance, and a *compostela*, a certificate of accomplishment, was given to them on completing the Way. Today, to earn the *compostela*, one needs to walk a minimum of 100 km or cycle at least 200 km.

At such times I'm glad I'm a Baptist!

However, *Saga* offers tourists a far more comfortable alternative. They can ride there in a luxury coach and stay in the five-star hotel nearby. One newspaper called it 'A Pampered Pilgrim's Progress'.

A shocking sermon

Now, no one reading Jesus' Sermon on the Mount could ever feel pampered. But they will feel challenged and even shocked (Matthew 5 – 7). When he was engaged in translating the New Testament into modern English, J. B. Phillips said that in the course of doing so, 'again and again the writer felt rather like an electrician rewiring an ancient house without being able to turn the mains off'![1]

The Sermon on the Mount certainly has that electric quality about it: at one time flooding us with light and warmth, and at other times sharply jolting us out of our complacency and carelessness. If any collection of words and sayings shows us the likeness of Christ, it is this one. It is all about us, and yet it is also all about him: he is its author and best exponent; this is the way he is and lives, and this is the way we must be, and the kind of life we must live.

This teaching is about life in the kingdom of God, that is, life under the rule of God (which is what 'the kingdom' means). The earliest message of Jesus, as of John, was that the kingdom of heaven, the kingdom of God, was at hand, and that the long centuries of waiting were over. Now God was doing a new thing in the world, beginning the rule of God, the reign of grace, and the day of salvation that would spread throughout the world.

And its sign would be the message and the lives of Jesus' followers. They would be different: God's new community, with different standards, motivations and power, a counter-culture proclaiming the future of God and already living in its new freedom, with lives touched by its grace. Now God was beginning his rule in the world, which brings redemption, renewal and eternal life.

This is your life

The Sermon on the Mount is not a taunting ideal that we can never reach, or a legal standard leaving us without hope of heaven. Rather, Jesus is preaching the presence of the kingdom of God, the principles that govern it and the powers at work within it. And men and women enter it in the faith of Jesus: he is the Door, the Way and the Saviour. He is the King who cannot be separated from the kingdom, the Son of God who leads the people of God; to belong to him is to belong to this kingdom. And those who belong to it discover working within them the life of the kingdom, the rule of God: humbling, softening, and transforming their lives, working not by imposition from outside, but by transformation from the inside.

It is important to see this in the opening Beatitudes:

Blessed are the poor in spirit,
   for theirs is the kingdom of heaven . . .
Blessed are the meek,
   for they will inherit the earth . . .
Blessed are those who hunger and thirst for
      righteousness,
   for they will be filled . . .
Blessed are those who are persecuted because
      of righteousness,
   for theirs is the kingdom of heaven.
(Matthew 5:3–10)

The Beatitudes are not a cloud of hazy ideals or even merely challenging possibilities. It is true that they do challenge us, and they do contain possibilities that unfold as the life of faith is matured and perfected. Yet they are descriptions of every child of the kingdom, and of that child from the first moment of the new birth 'from above' (John 3:3, NRSV).

The Sermon on the Mount describes our identity and defines the new life at work within us: what we are now, as well as what we must strive more and more to be. It is about the bent of our souls and the direction of our lives. It is, in fact, the deepest truth about us. It is not a romantic ideal constantly out of our reach, or a wistful vision of what we could be, or a series of exclusion clauses in a gospel that is for everyone except us. Nor is it about an artificial life of iron discipline.

The Sermon on the Mount is about the life we share with Jesus, about the true nature and real implications of what has happened to us, and about the kind of people we are and are becoming. It monitors the heartbeat of our new life, the new power at work within us. It displays the working life of the Holy Spirit who lives in us, whose great work is to conform us to God and the image of his Son, and so to transform these already-saved lives of ours: 'You are the salt of the earth . . . You are the light of the world. A town built on a hill cannot be hidden' (Matthew 5:13–14).

If we fail to reckon with this, then we will never see ourselves in the Sermon on the Mount, and what is more, we will never find joy or hope or 'home' in it. But the whole point is that it *is* home, and we *are* there, and there *is* hope: new life is expanding 'from one degree of glory to another' (2 Corinthians 3:18, NRSV).

Of course, all this will be missed if the Sermon on the Mount is separated from the gospel of the cross and resurrection, and from the truth of justification by faith alone. And it is indeed missed: by the poet, the humanist and the politician, who only want to find expression in it for their romantic idealism or secular humanism or as a convenient escape route. I recall an example of this from my boyhood in Wales.

The mind boggles!

When I was a boy we had a witty but irreverent Welsh journalist who wrote an amusing and clever article on the common phrase: 'the imagination boggles'. He said something like this: 'Now why is it that we say, "the imagination boggles"? We use the word of no other part. Nothing ever "boggles" except the imagination. It seems that this is its particular attribute or province to "boggle".'

And as this was easier to experience than to describe, he would tell his readers how to make it happen. 'Write down', he would say, 'some astonishing statement, such as, "Income tax reduced to five pence in the pound!" or "The meek will inherit the earth – next Wednesday!"' Then, he said, you would experience your imagination 'boggling'.

To this writer, the idea of such an airy-fairy virtue as meekness being brought down to earth was 'mind-boggling'. So it has always been. In Jesus' time the meek were the very last people who expected to inherit anything, but God says they will inherit *everything*. They were not able to stand aggressively, even for their rights, yet they would inherit the earth in the day of Christ's coming. And the earth they would inherit would be a far better place than the earth so many strive to grab.

Jesus says, 'Blessed are the poor in spirit', and the world says, 'Blessed are the loud, the proud, the heard.' Jesus says, 'Blessed are the meek, for they will inherit the earth', and the world says, 'You must be joking!' Jesus says, 'Blessed are those who mourn', and the world goes to a party.

Unworthy but undaunted

Within ourselves, however, there is still the old life of the world as well as the new life of the kingdom. Jesus says, 'Do not store up for yourselves treasures on earth . . . But store up for yourselves treasures in heaven' (Matthew 6:19–20). But if he asks us where most of our energies and ambitions lie, we answer with downcast eyes and burning cheeks, for this sermon humbles us, even if it does not condemn us.

There is pride as well as poverty of spirit in us, apathy as well as hunger for God's way, double-mindedness as well as purity of heart, and cowardice as well as loyalty. Though we are not what we used to be, we are not yet all that we shall be. Jesus says, 'Do not judge . . . first take the plank out of your own eye' (Matthew 7:1–5), but often we do not hear him because we are so busy taking specks from each other's eyes – yes, even in the churches!

This is Jesus' manifesto, and it stands against so much of what we see in fallen human society. But we must stand alongside him against its proud pretensions and corrupt self-serving, bearing the mockery and the resentment that is always attached to the rule of God. For to those already saved by grace, it is the map, the compass and the companion of our walk to heaven. Here is the life of true freedom, the way of happiness, the straight road home.

Future shock

It is true that there is a clear emphasis on the future: 'Blessed are those who mourn, for they will be comforted . . . Blessed are the merciful, for they will be shown mercy . . . Blessed are the pure in heart, for they will see God . . . Blessed are you when people insult you, persecute you and falsely say all kinds of evil against you because of me . . . because great is your reward in heaven.'

But this future has already begun. Since the resurrection of Jesus, the end has already arrived! The rule of God has begun and is visible in our lives – a sign to the world of what God is now doing. The victory of Christ is behind us, and the future of Christ is before us!

This sermon shows the character of our Father in heaven: he is good and does good. It is his character that should shape our church communities into places of acceptance and encouragement and good counsel. Followers of Jesus learn to act and react as he taught and modelled. If we fall, there must be those in the church who pick us up; if we forget, there must be those who remind us; if we get tired, there must be those who congratulate and encourage us. This is the transforming power at work within us all as followers of Christ, and it will end in breathtaking conformity to his image.

This transformation is not the work of an hour, but of a lifetime. It meets all sorts of impediments, difficulties and challenges – in us as well as around us. And so for a while it co-exists with contrary forces, sinful instincts and the awkward structures of a fallen world. (We shall look at these in Part 4.) But Jesus calls us to 'a safe place' even in the midst of conflict, from which to 'wrestle and toil and pray', and that safe place is himself, his character and his commitment to us.

Called to a safe place

Jesus says, 'Come to me, all you who are weary and burdened, and I will give you rest, for I am *gentle* [meek] and *humble* in heart' (Matthew 11:29, italics mine).

The one theme that binds together the whole character and activity of the Son of God, from his incarnation through public ministry to his sacrificial death, is self-giving love, and in that love he is 'gentle and humble in heart'. Leon Morris observes:

In heart locates these qualities at the centre of his being. It was not that he pretended to be humble and made a show of being lowly: he really was lowly, and that at the very centre of all that he was. Because of what he is in his innermost being, meek and lowly, those who come to him *find rest*.[2]

It was this character that pitied the crowds who came to him as sheep without a shepherd (Matthew 9:36), that welcomed the children (19:13–15) and raised the fallen (Luke 7:38).

Indeed, it is this very claim that attracts the weary and burdened whom he calls to himself. Who would ever bring their burdens to someone who was cocky and self-confident? Who would bring their failures to someone who was only interested in success stories? And who would bring their sins to a proud Pharisee who wouldn't touch a sinner? But a Son of God who was gentle and humble in heart – now, you would feel safe with someone like that. This meekness is not weakness; it is strength under control.

The place of forgiveness

At the heart of the Sermon on the Mount is the Lord's Prayer, and at the heart of that prayer is the petition: 'Forgive us our debts, as we also have forgiven our debtors.' On both the national and personal fronts there are few more urgent matters in our world today.

The community of the forgiven must be one of forgiveness. We, of all people, need to show each other the love that bears all things and believes all things and hopes all things (1 Corinthians 13:7). When a fellow believer has been short with you, you do not know the strains they may be under; when they react harshly, you should respond gently; when they act out of character, love should give the benefit of the doubt; and when their faith is low, they need your prayers more than ever. In the matter of forgiveness for personal injury by a fellow Christian, I often quote some words by Elisabeth Elliot, spoken at a Spring Harvest address years ago: 'You can either stand with Satan against that person, or you can stand with Christ for them.'

The Hebrew noun *satan* means an 'adversary', and the verb *satan* also means 'to accuse'. Satan is called 'the accuser' of God's people (see Revelation 12:10); do we really want to stand alongside him in accusation?

There are people who have never worked a miracle, but who *are* a miracle. We may not be able to work miracles, but we can do something that is far more significant and telling: we can love on where love has been forfeited; we can forgive where forgiveness is not deserved; we can be reconciled where reconciliation seemed impossible. And the watching world can be drawn a little nearer to God.

There are many who have in their memory serious injuries: physical and sexual abuse in childhood; betrayal and abandonment in marriage; gossip, rumour and slander at work or in the neighbourhood; and the loss of respect or promotion. The list is endless even before we come to the petty quarrels or differences that can mar fellowship in the local church.

Some of the most useful treatments of this theme are found in Dr R. T. Kendall's books: *Total Forgiveness*, *Tales of Total Forgiveness* (with Julia Fisher) and *Totally Forgiving Ourselves*.[3]

Again and again, those who pass through these fires testify to the overwhelming peace and joy that often come as a breath from heaven, an early 'Well done, good and faithful servant!' (Matthew 25:23). Many have found themselves released from poisoning bitterness, preoccupation and anger, freed to go on in life into the future of God, leaving behind the injustices, pain and indignation.

For some the peace of forgiveness is immediate, for others gradual, and indeed for some it may be a lifetime's steady work. But never be discouraged: you are succeeding every day just by battling with it and praying on: 'Father, forgive us our sins, as we forgive those who sin against us.'

To refuse to forgive is to forget what Christ has done for us. Jesus himself expressed in words of prayer as men were nailing him to the cross what that act of atonement was all about: 'Father, forgive them, for they do not know what they are doing' (Luke 23:34). Where others screamed curses, he prayed forgiveness; where others begged for themselves, he begged for his tormentors. Moreover, he did so in unconstrained love, and with no need of personal forgiveness. In this too he was the Son of his Father, the perfect image of God – and this is the likeness he wants to increase in us.

However, there are other levels of forgiveness which most of us have never had to face. Sometimes the depth of cruelty, loss and forgiveness is far beyond our experience, or even our sight. And the effect on others in the watching world is also incalculable.

That was the case with Gladys Staines, the wife of the Australian missionary Graham Staines. In January 1999 millions in India saw and heard her on television, in programme after programme, as she forgave the cruel mob of militant Hindus who had set fire to her husband's camper van. Graham and their two young sons, Philip (aged ten) and Timothy (aged eight), were sleeping in the van and were burned to death. Afterwards Gladys continued to work with the poor of Orissa for six more years.

The foot-washing

There was one incident where Jesus illustrated his character, his values and his love in a way that has never been forgotten:

> The evening meal [the Passover] was in progress, and the
> devil had already prompted Judas, the son of Simon Iscariot,
> to betray Jesus. Jesus knew that the Father had put all things
> under his power, and that he had come from God and was
> returning to God.
> (John 13:2–3)

The drama is intense. Against the multiple backgrounds –
satanic powers closing in, one of his own disciples betraying
him, his own divine identity and destiny as Lord of heaven
and earth, and his approaching death – what does Jesus do?

Calmly, deliberately and silently at first, it seems:

> he got up from the meal, took off his outer clothing, and
> wrapped a towel round his waist. After that, he poured water
> into a basin and began to wash his disciples' feet, drying them
> with the towel that was wrapped round him.
> (verses 4–5)

It was the job of the lowliest servant, and no one wanted to
do it. But Jesus did it. We live in a society where everyone is
insisting on their rights, but Jesus is King of a society where
people are prepared to give up their rights for others. In his
upside-down kingdom the greatest are the servers, and
greatness is in serving, and indeed serving not those who are
eminent, but those who have no status and can give no reward.

This is the kind of leadership Jesus models, the kind of
service he loves to, and will, reward in the coming age of the
kingdom.

Self-sacrifice used to be seen as the supreme virtue; now it
is often regarded more as a vice, or at least a waste, a baffling
miscalculation. Now all the talk is of self-discovery and self-
development, not self-sacrifice or even service. But in fact,

self-sacrifice is at the heart of family and marriage and parent-hood, and much else besides, including at the heart of Christian communities, as we noted earlier. Jesus did not say, 'I have washed your feet, and now you must wash mine.' We would all line up if that were the case! Instead, he says to us all, 'I have washed your feet / I have died for your sins / I have washed your soul – now serve others as I have served you. Now love others as I have loved you.'

Of course, there are things involved in this that are unique to Jesus Christ. You and I cannot die for anyone's sins. We cannot even make atonement for our own. But there are some ways in which we can be like the Lord Jesus, things we are commanded to do that show we belong to him: 'Now that I, your Lord and Teacher, have washed your feet, you also should wash one another's feet' (verse 14).

This is living in the supernatural: choosing to be a servant in a world where everyone wants to be the master, the top dog, the admired. This is the demonstration to the world that we serve a living Christ, that we know a loving God, that we draw strength from the Spirit of God who lives within us and helps us. This is conversion, the turning around of a life, the regeneration of a heart, the transformation of a character. This is Christlikeness. And it matters hugely.

6

The Suffering Servant and suffering Christians

Some years ago, Ken Matthews of Jesmond Parish Church, Newcastle, posted this fascinating story on the web:

A friend of mine was speaking on a University mission a few years back. He took some time off to get his hair cut mid-way through the week and got into conversation with the hairdresser. It started off as a kind of 'you're not from round here?' sort of conversation, but pretty soon he was asked what he was doing in the area. My friend mentioned that he was doing a mission at St. Andrews University. 'A mission?' said the hairdresser, 'that's a Christian thing isn't it?'

Now you're never sure whether to own up to being a Christian when someone has a pair of scissors at your throat, but my friend took a gulp and said 'Yes.' At which point the hairdresser told him that he'd just become a Christian recently himself, and went on to give him the full story. He'd been working at a different hair salon with a girl who was a Christian herself. She was always polite, ever so helpful, charming and kind to everyone who came in, and was for ever inviting him to come to church with her. He always managed to find a reason to politely decline, until one morning she came in all bright and breezy after he had had a pretty heavy night of it the evening before. She invited him to a special event at church at the weekend and something inside him just snapped. He felt a distinct urge to persecute her.

Now I don't know how you persecute someone in a hairdressers, but I'm pretty sure I've been a victim myself on a number of occasions. For this guy it sufficed for him to turn over her chair, slap her hard across the face and storm out of the salon. He was at home later that night when the phone rang. It was her. She said, 'You didn't answer my question about whether you wanted to come to church this weekend.' He didn't have the heart to say no. He went, heard what he said was the most wonderful news ever – that Jesus had died for sinners like him – and he gave his life to Jesus there and then.[1]

Following Jesus into hostile territory

If we become followers of Christ, we will find his footsteps taking us into hostile territory. Jesus prepared his followers for every kind of suffering:

If the world hates you, keep in mind that it hated me first. If you belonged to the world, it would love you as its own. As it is, you do not belong to the world, but I have chosen you out of the world. That is why the world hates you. Remember what I told you: 'A servant is not greater than his master.' If they persecuted me, they will persecute you also. If they obeyed my teaching, they will obey yours also. They will treat you this way because of my name, for they do not know the one who sent me.

(John 15:18–21)

'The world' in John's Gospel is a term used to describe a society organized to keep God out of its affairs. And as individuals too, people do not want God interfering with their preferred choices and priorities. You and I used to be like that, but we have left the world's ranks and gone over to the enemy! Where we are known for our allegiance to God, we are now an uncomfortable reminder of him, and when we speak of his Son Jesus Christ, we are likely to arouse antagonism. No Christian has fully experienced identification with Christ who has not openly confessed him to others who do not know him, and suffered for it in some way. This may come in the form of embarrassment at their mockery, disadvantage and loss as a result of their prejudice, or simply disappointment and sorrow in the face of their rejection of the Son of God.

One-track people!

The apostle Peter offers the same warning and encouragement in his first letter:

> To this you were called, because Christ suffered for you,
> leaving you an example, that you should follow in his steps.
>
> He committed no sin,
>   and no deceit was found in his mouth.
>
> When they hurled their insults at him, he did not retaliate; when he suffered, he made no threats. Instead, he entrusted himself to him who judges justly. 'He himself bore our sins' in his body on the cross, so that we might die to sins and live for righteousness; 'by his wounds you have been healed.'
> (1 Peter 2:21–24)

It's important to take our model, our standards, our pattern not from others or from our own previous efforts, but from Christ, as Peter puts it, following his footsteps whatever direction they take, whatever terrain they pass through. Karen Jobes comments:

> This is a strong image associating the Christian's life with the life of Christ. For one cannot step into the footsteps of Jesus and head off in any other direction than the direction he took, and his footsteps lead to the cross, through the grave, and onward to glory.[2]

Followers of Jesus are in this sense one-track people. And where did they learn to forgive even their persecutors? From the one who, as his persecutors were crucifying him, prayed, 'Father, forgive them, for they do not know what they are doing' (Luke 23:34). So again, in the words of the second-century Church Father Tertullian, 'The blood of the martyrs is the seed of the church.'[3]

When insult is honour, and shame is glory

Later Peter urges them to defeat surprise and self-pity with joy and reassurance:

> Dear friends, do not be surprised at the fiery ordeal that has come on you to test you, as though something strange were happening to you. But rejoice inasmuch as you participate in the sufferings of Christ, so that you may be overjoyed when his glory is revealed. If you are insulted because of the name of Christ, you are blessed, for the Spirit of glory and of God rests on you.
>
> (1 Peter 4:12–14)

What a reversal of the world's values! Insult for Jesus' sake means honour, and loss for Jesus is gain, 'for the Spirit of glory and of God rests on you'.

John Piper refers to the time when Muhammad was portrayed in twelve cartoons in the Danish newspaper *Jyllands-Posten*:

> The uproar across the Muslim world was intense and sometimes violent. Flags were burned, embassies were torched, and at least one Christian church was stoned. The cartoonists went into hiding in fear for their lives, like Salman Rushdie before them . . . The caricature and mockery of Christ has continued to this day. Martin Scorsese portrayed Jesus in *The Last Temptation of Christ* as wracked with doubt and beset with sexual lust. Andres Serrano was funded by the National Endowment for the Arts to portray Jesus on a cross sunk in a bottle of urine. *The Da Vinci Code* portrays Jesus as a mere mortal who married and fathered children.

And then he asks and answers the burning question: 'How should his followers respond?' His response might surprise us all:

> If Christ had not been insulted, there would be no salvation. This was his saving work: to be insulted and die to rescue sinners from the wrath of God . . . That's the most basic difference between Christ and Muhammad and between a Muslim and a follower of Christ. For Christ, enduring the mockery of the cross was the essence of his mission. And for a true follower of Christ, enduring suffering patiently for the glory of Christ is the essence of obedience. 'Blessed are you when others revile you and persecute you and utter all kinds of evil against you falsely on my account' (Matthew 5:11).

During his life on earth Jesus was called a bastard (John 8:41), a drunkard (Matthew 11:19), a blasphemer (Matthew 26:65), a devil (Matthew 10:25); and he promised his followers the same: 'If they have called the master of the house Beelzebul, how much more will they malign those of his household' (Matthew 10:25).

How should we respond? Piper replies:

On the one hand, we are grieved and angered. On the other hand, we identify with Christ, and embrace his suffering, and rejoice in our afflictions, and say with the apostle Paul that vengeance belongs to the Lord, let us love our enemies and win them with the gospel. If Christ did his work by being insulted, we must do ours likewise.[4]

People who dance to another tune

Our Lord Jesus said:

Blessed are you when people insult you, persecute you and falsely say all kinds of evil against you because of me. Rejoice and be glad, because great is your reward in heaven, for in the same way they persecuted the prophets before you.
(Matthew 5:11–12)

His word for 'rejoice' here is a strong one: 'leap for joy', 'rejoice greatly', and that is the word which Peter uses when he says, 'rejoice inasmuch as you participate in the sufferings of Christ' (1 Peter 4:13). It is of course an extraordinary thing to say, frankly, and a strange defiance of sight and feeling and loss and pain. Yet they did it – and their testimony to Jesus convicted their very persecutors. In courts of law, in prisons, in poverty, in disgrace for Jesus Christ, these early Christians could feel the triumph of their faith and anticipate their share of Christ's praise and glory and honour in the future. To share Jesus' inheritance, writes Thomas A. Smail, 'is to enter into his unique combination of obedience and authority, humility and greatness, weakness and power, suffering and glory, dying and rising, serving and reigning'.[5]

Pray for the persecuted church

Careful research estimates that the number of Christian martyrs in the twentieth century was about one million. From South America to Northern Asia, from Mexico to Rwanda, from the Sudan to Pakistan, in Communist Russia and China and in countries under Nazi occupation, Christians have been imprisoned, tortured and put to death for their faith as followers of Jesus Christ and their refusal to exchange his lordship for any other. The twenty-first century, in its first decades, has seen a grim history of Christian churches burned, and Christians killed, raped or kidnapped, in Africa, Asia and the Middle East. (Follow the literature of the Barnabas Fund, Christian Solidarity Worldwide or Open Doors and other such organizations to keep your prayers abreast of world events.)

When thousands of Christians fled his city in Iraq, one civil servant, who had to abandon his home, said, 'We left everything behind us. We took only our souls.' As I write this, hundreds of thousands of Christians are being displaced from Syria and Iraq, and living in camps in Lebanon and elsewhere because of their Christian identity.

However, people are turning to Christ in the very situations where state persecution rages around the world. In Iraq, moderate Muslims are turning to Christ as IS violence rages. In Algeria, there has been enormous growth in the church, especially among the Kabyle Berbers. In Iran, the authorities appear to be struggling to prevent the huge growth of Christianity, and China is soon likely to be the country with the world's largest Christian population. But the cost of all this is always the courage and suffering of Christ's people, and their willingness to forgive even their persecutors – sometimes to the astonishment of their neighbours. David Garrison's book *A Wind in the House of Islam*[6] gathers testimonies and statistics from Muslim countries across the world, showing an unprecedented turning to Christ among Muslims, often against a background of repression, conflict and disillusionment.

Paul and the cost of following Christ

Let's look at a New Testament example of suffering. The apostle Paul was told by the risen Christ from the beginning that he would suffer many things for him (Acts 9:16), and eighteen years later Paul would feel forced by his critics to enumerate his sufferings for Christ in his second letter to the Corinthians. First, he indicates the cost in general: 'As servants of God we commend ourselves in every way: in great endurance; in troubles, hardships and distresses' (2 Corinthians 6:4).

Paul did not have an easy ministry or one that was widely applauded. He fulfilled the commission the risen Christ had given to him as an evangelist and church planter in the Roman world through 'a blizzard of troubles', as the Church Father Chrysostom put it. We can read some of the story in Acts and some in this letter, but only Christ knew the full version (Acts 9:16).

He needed endurance to keep up his extraordinary ministry as an evangelist, church planter, teacher and pastor. In his long, hard journeys from city to city it has been calculated that the apostle Paul travelled at least 12,000 miles on foot in the years recorded in Acts, as well as perhaps 2,000 or 3,000 more after the account in Acts closes, going as far west as Spain, which was in his plan (Romans 15:23–24).[7]

In the years preceding that, he had spent another thirteen years or so evangelizing in Arabia, Cilicia and Syria, before he came to Antioch where the account of his travels in Acts begins. This probably brings the total number of miles travelled, mainly on foot, to well over 20,000. Endurance indeed!

He speaks further of 'troubles, hardships and distresses' (2 Corinthians 6:4). 'Troubles' would have included bouts of illness, including his 'thorn in the flesh', and the word translated 'distresses' might be rendered 'tight corners' or 'dire straits'.[8] With long days of travel, sometimes through harsh and lonely terrain, it was a hard and sometimes dangerous way of life. That was the cost of Paul's ministry in general.

Paul goes on to indicate the cost of it in more detail: 'in beatings, imprisonments and riots' (verse 5). Of the beatings he could say later in this letter: 'I have . . . been flogged more severely, and been exposed to death again and again. Five times I received from the Jews the forty lashes minus one. Three times I was beaten with rods' (2 Corinthians 11:23b–25a).

Of the imprisonments he says he has 'been in prison more frequently' (2 Corinthians 11:23) than any of his critics. An early Church Father, Clement Bishop of Rome, writing at about the end of the first century, says that Paul was in chains on seven occasions,[9] and in Acts we learn of two longer imprisonments: two years in Caesarea and two in Rome, leading to his first trial in Rome (Acts 24 – 28).

The book of Acts records eight riots stirred up against Paul and the young churches: in Antioch of Pisidia, Iconium,

Lystra, Philippi, Thessalonica, Corinth, Ephesus and Jerusalem. Almost everywhere he goes, there is trouble, but it is gospel trouble: trouble not caused by the gospel, but by hatred of it and opposition to it.

Paul adds to his involuntary sufferings some of his more voluntary ones: hard work, sleepless nights and hunger (see 2 Corinthians 11:27). These probably all refer to his unwearied efforts. There were his days of manual labour as a leather worker and tent-repairer, working deep into the night in order to support his teaching sessions and not be a financial burden to anyone. There was also pastoral involvement, counselling (Acts 20:31) and nights of prayer. It does not add up to a first-class ticket through life, does it?

So Paul reminds his critics of the cost he paid to bring the gospel to others and to them. Earlier he had told the Galatian believers, 'Let no one cause me trouble, for I bear on my body the marks of Jesus' (Galatians 6:17). His back had become a map criss-crossed with the marks of old beatings for Christ.

A present-day martyr for Christ

Twenty centuries on, and the line has grown to many hundreds of thousands following Jesus, carrying their cross to their own place of execution. One of the most memorable testimonies of faith and forgiveness in modern times has been in Iran.

The Right Reverend Hassan Dehqani-Tafti was an Anglican bishop in Iran from 1961 to 1990. He spent the last ten years of his ministry, until he was eighty-seven, in exile following the 1979 revolution, and survived an attempt on his life in November of that year. In May of the following year his only son, twenty-four-year-old Bahram, was murdered, apparently by government agents. For Bahram's funeral he composed a prayer, the closing lines of which were:

> O God, Bahram's blood has multiplied the fruit of the Spirit in the soil of our souls; so when his murderers stand before Thee on the Day of Judgment, remember the fruit of the Spirit by which they have enriched our lives, and forgive.

One woman's story

Amy Carmichael was a missionary to orphans in India in the 1920s. She rescued hundreds of orphaned children – especially little girls who would be dedicated to Hindu gods for use in sexual temple rituals – and lovingly cared for each child God sent her. One day in 1931 she prayed, 'God, please do with me whatever you want. Do anything that will help me to serve you better.'

That very same day she fell, suffering fractures that would cripple her for the rest of her life. She was not one to be discouraged or bitter when faced with pain or persecution. While her growing children had continual freedom to enter her bedroom and share their hearts with their beloved 'mother', as they called her, she now had quiet times allowing her to write books, poems and letters that were translated and shared around the world. These words were precious to her: 'For it has been granted to you on behalf of Christ not only to believe in him, but also to suffer for him' (Philippians 1:29). Confined to her room, she preached to tens of thousands worldwide, then and now. One of her most famous poems is entitled 'No Scar?' Asking where are the scars we bear in the service of Christ, it is both searching and challenging to us comfortable Westerners with so few scars of our own to show.

It may mean suffering, persecution or even martyrdom, but we all as believers follow Jesus into hostile territory.

We have seen how Christ is our model of what Christlikeness looks like in our world, but he is not a model who mocks us, leaving us helpless and distanced. He has given us significant and enormous help in becoming more and more like him, and to some of these helps we now turn.

Part 3
The helps to Christlikeness

7

The Spirit of God

Why are you reading this book? Why are you interested in becoming Christlike? Perhaps you remember a time when you would not have thought of doing such a thing, much less valued it above everything else and wanted it for yourself. The answer above and beyond all others is because the Holy Spirit has been working in your life right up to this moment, giving you a new understanding of the things of God, new desires for eternal life with him and a new determination to follow Jesus Christ as your Lord and Saviour.

The Holy Spirit is the single and sufficient explanation for every Christian's life and faith. When you became a follower of Christ, it was the Holy Spirit who first enlightened your mind so that you began to understand as never before. It was the Spirit who moved your will so that you began to want what you had never wanted before. And it was the Spirit who touched your emotions so that you could sing with meaning, 'Love so amazing, so divine, demands my life, my soul, my all.'[1]

The Holy Spirit is God-next-to-us. Every time we hear God speaking in sensitivity and faith, it is the Spirit who is working.

Every time we respond to God's love in the gospel with joy and faithful obedience, it is the Spirit who is drawing, enabling and blessing us. Every time we take the good news about Jesus to others with courage and love, it is the Spirit who is moving out into the world – through us!

The Holy Spirit makes us more like Jesus

We are going to look at the role of the Holy Spirit before focusing on the fruits of the Spirit. The apostle Paul repeatedly speaks of Jesus dying to release us from the *power* of sin as well as from the *penalty* of sin (Romans 6:14). But what is the link between what we are to do now and what Christ did then? What is the link between his atoning death and our power to live for God? The answer again is the Holy Spirit. Jesus Christ has won the right to give us the Spirit of God to be an indwelling Spirit, helping us, sanctifying us, giving us power to resist sin and to follow righteousness. This is one of the principal fruits of his death: he has won the right to turn sinners into saints (John 17:19; Ephesians 5:25–27; Titus 2:14; 1 Peter 2:24).

In his classic book *Holiness*, J. C. Ryle insists:

> He who supposes that Jesus Christ only lived and died and rose again in order to provide justification and forgiveness of sins for His people, has yet much to learn. Whether he knows it or not, he is dishonouring our blessed Lord and making Him only a half Saviour. The Lord Jesus has undertaken everything that His people's souls require: not only to deliver them from the guilt of their sins, by His atoning death; but from the dominion of their sins, by placing in their hearts the Holy Spirit; not only to justify them – but also to sanctify them. He is, thus, not only their 'righteousness,' but their 'sanctification' (1 Cor. 1:30).[2]

Why, in particular, is he called the Holy Spirit when the Father and the Son are also holy? One answer often given is that his great work in the world is to make men and women holy. Sanctification is not merely a matter of keeping rules; it is a close walk with God the Holy Spirit. He writes the law of God on our hearts, deepens our understanding of what is good in God's sight, sensitizes our consciences when we sin and encourages us in every good work. We are saved by grace, but grace evokes gratitude, and the Christian life is one of grateful response to an undeserved love.

It has been well said that 'It is the Spirit's ministry to bring the sinner to the Saviour and to make the sinner like the Saviour.'

> And we all, who with unveiled faces contemplate the
> Lord's glory, are being transformed into his image with
> ever-increasing glory, which comes from the Lord, who is
> the Spirit.
> (2 Corinthians 3:18)

The everyday Christ

The Holy Spirit delights to work with us in our daily life and our ordinary involvements and encounters. He knows the opportunities that will come our way to grow in the likeness of Christ: the needs we will encounter, the difficult people we will meet, the highs and the lows of experience, the tests and the encouragements of faith. He is there before us and here within us, strengthening and guiding us as we develop in the life of prayer, as we absorb the Word of God, and as we engage with the people of God. He is the God of all encouragement, and he produces in us the likeness of Christ as the fruit of the Spirit: 'the fruit of the Spirit is love, joy, peace, forbearance, kindness, goodness, faithfulness, gentleness and self-control' (Galatians 5:22–23).

But all this takes time.

Seeds for sale

The story is told of a woman who has a dream where she wanders into a shop and finds Jesus behind a counter. Jesus says, 'You can have anything your heart desires.' Astonished but delighted, she asks for peace, joy, happiness, wisdom and freedom from fear. Then she adds, 'Not just for me, but for the whole earth.' Jesus smiles and says, 'I think you misunderstand me. We don't sell fruits, only seeds.'[3]

We all want to be more like Jesus, to see more of the fruit of the Spirit in our own lives and in the lives of others. But it does not come in boxes, full-grown, but in a thousand days and prayers and deeds which water and grow seeds planted by the Holy Spirit when he first came into the heart.

Notice there that it is the fruit (singular) of the Spirit, not fruits in the plural. The new life comes as a whole: it is all there in embryonic form and it grows with use and exercise. It is not possible to pick and choose some of these things here and leave others. That is because the character of Christ which is being formed in us is not some of these, but all of them.

The fruit of the Spirit

The first-named fruit is:

Love

The fruit of the Spirit is love. And as we know from chapter 3, God's love is not just an attitude, but an action. It is his self-giving activity in which he reaches out in blessing to sustain, help and guide us. The height of God's love is seen in the death of his Son for our salvation: 'For God so loved the world that he gave his one and only Son' (John 3:16). In all eternity there will never be a greater demonstration of love than that. Integral to this was the self-giving of the Son who 'loved us and gave himself up for us as a fragrant offering and sacrifice to God' (Ephesians 5:2). Each of us now can speak of the Son of God 'who loved me and gave himself for me' (Galatians 2:20), and the Lord Jesus tells us, as he told the Twelve, 'My command is this: love each other as I have loved you' (John 15:12).

You can see just how far this is from mere sentimentality. If this is love in God, then it tells us something about true love in us: not just a warm feeling, but a willed commitment to one another, something that transcends moods and survives disagreements. This love comes from God, makes us more like God, and it loves like God. God loved us even when he was angry towards us because of our sin. He did not love us because we were worthy or loveable, and we too must learn to love even those we find hard to love.

We saw earlier that Christian churches especially must be communities of love. As oil in the engine of your car, so love is 'liquid engineering' in the church. It prevents our personalities rubbing, our gifts grating and our zeal overheating and bringing everything to a halt.

Essentially, this first part of the Spirit's fruit says it all, and all else flows from it.

Joy

At the heart of God there is infinite and immeasurable joy: Father, Son and Holy Spirit have lived in love and joy from all eternity. And God's love will one day take us up into his joy. Jesus expressed overflowing joy as he contemplated the spread of the kingdom of God through the preaching of the gospel and its effects in a needy world (Luke 10:21–24). He faced the cross, strengthened by the joy that was set before him: his place at the right hand of God as the Saviour King of millions in an eternal kingdom (Hebrews 12:2).

That joy is shared by all who take their part in the spread of the gospel. Even now it is the early work of the Holy Spirit to make God's joy the fuel of our lives. If it were not so, then Christian life and service would simply become teeth-gritting determination, wearing and unwelcome. Joy kept Paul going despite all his hardships: he is the apostle of joy. The word occurs more often in his letters than anywhere else in the New Testament – twenty-one times in fact!

Like love, this joy transcends moods and personality types. It comes when there is a deep sense of the presence of God in one's life. And because of that awareness, we can rejoice in God when we cannot rejoice in anything else, that is, in hard times and even deeply sad ones. 'Joy', said C. S. Lewis famously, 'is the serious business of heaven.'[4]

Are you cultivating joy in your own life and sharing it with others?

Peace

This peace is not the condition of a brain deadened with tranquillizers, nor is it a natural state developed by exercises in meditation. Rather, it is peace with God through our Lord Jesus Christ and the recognition of his friendship, his favour and his future. Jesus said, 'Peace I leave with you; my peace I give you. I do not give to you as the world gives' (John 14:27). He could not give what he did not have, but having it, he shared it.

This peace comes from a settled assurance of salvation: God is no longer feared but trusted; this life is no longer all there is, and its burdens can be borne and its gains held loosely as a result. Out of that relationship of forgiveness and peace there grows a whole and sound person. The biblical words for peace mean just that: wholeness, soundness, completeness. God's peace is the antidote to exhausting ambition and paralysing despair alike.

Patience

The word for patience in the original Greek text might be better translated as 'longsuffering', as in the King James Version. We do not have quite the right word: F. F. Bruce suggests that if there was a term in English like 'long-tempered' to counterbalance 'short-tempered', we might be near to what we have here. We marvel, as we read the Gospels, at Jesus' patience with his disciples in their short-sightedness and rivalry and personal failures. This is because Jesus is long-tempered, and we are not – at least not yet, but hopefully we are on the way. We must become strongly weak, refusing to retaliate when we are misunderstood, or to rubbish others when we are not heeded.

The fifth and sixth words in Paul's list (kindness and goodness) belong together.

Kindness and goodness

The word 'kindness' in Scripture refers to the goodness and generosity of God to all humankind, exercised with forbearance and patience, often in the teeth of ingratitude and injustice. Jesus said our heavenly Father sends his sun and rain and other blessings on the righteous and the unrighteous, so we too must exercise love and mercy and generous kindness to all, 'especially to those who are of the household of faith' (Galatians 6:10, ESV). The sheer goodness of God urges us to share our good things with generosity and joy. No one was ever kinder than Jesus, who fed the hungry, healed the sick, welcomed children and didn't turn sinners away. And he said, 'Go and do likewise' (Luke 10:37).

Now, anyone can do some of these things some of the time, but it is a characteristic of the Spirit's work that he grows in us the fruit of faithfulness or dependability.

Faithfulness

God is faithful, and his faithfulness is the stability of our lives:

> He is the Rock, his works are perfect,
> and all his ways are just.
> A faithful God who does no wrong,
> upright and just is he.
> (Deuteronomy 32:4)

Jesus preached two parables to illustrate the importance of this quality in the lives of those entrusted with the gospel: the parable of the talents (Matthew 25:14–30) and the parable of the ten minas (Luke 19:11–27). We must be faithful stewards of what has been entrusted to us by God, seeking to serve him faithfully wherever we are. Christ Jesus is our model, and he demonstrates that this quality is valued by God in our daily lives, however 'ordinary' they may be: 'Whoever can be trusted with very little can also be trusted with much' (Luke 16:10).

One of the most important words in the Old Testament is 'covenant'. In the ancient world a covenant was a special kind of undertaking, agreement or treaty, usually ratified by an oath. In the Old Testament God used this form of undertaking to impress upon his people the dependability of his solemn word or promise (e.g. Genesis 15:12–21; 17:1–14; Jeremiah 31:31–34). And God's love is covenant love.

Someone once defined covenant love as 'abandoning the option to quit'. That is a good line for friendships, churches and families – abandoning the option to quit. And it is God's bottom line with us: his loyal love refuses to abandon his people even when the relationship is under great strain. Likeness to Christ will always include faithfulness, and the Spirit will always work to make it a priority in our lives so that others find us dependable.

Gentleness

We sometimes hear of 'assertiveness classes' today, and there are indeed individuals who need to attend them. But most of us probably have a greater need for classes in gentleness or 'meekness'. Both Moses and Jesus are described in these terms: neither was weak, but neither was wild either. Jesus said:

> Come to me, all you who are weary and burdened, and I will give you rest. Take my yoke upon you and learn from me, for I am gentle and humble in heart, and you will find rest for your souls. For my yoke is easy and my burden is light.
> (Matthew 11:28–30)

The weary and burdened came to Jesus, as to a safe place, and they will only come to us if we too are safe: not brittle and unpredictable, but gentle and humble in heart. The gentle person is the one who will get nearest to the heart of another to hear their secret regrets and speak words of wisdom and hope into their lives. We need to be accountable to one another, but gentleness can take the sting even out of necessary reproof.

Churches must be characterized by gentleness and good will if they are to keep in step with the Spirit and remain communities of shared faith and love. Some people are quick to take offence, and they put everyone else on the defensive. Let us aim to cultivate churches of gentle people: not those who are weak or insipid, but strong people who combine strength with tenderness.

Self-control

Self-control is last on the list. The word was especially used with regard to the passions of human nature and in connection with sexual morality, something that we will look at in a later chapter in 'Facing the contradictions within ourselves'. Jesus spoke very clearly about sexual temptation in his analysis of the human heart and its sin (Mark 7:20–23).

Few things ruin a life like sexual promiscuity, or wreck a marriage like sexual betrayal, or damage a church like sexual scandal. The context of Paul's teaching is that many of the new Christians had come out of a Roman Gentile world of considerable immorality. There were still plenty of temptations to guard against. But Christ had died to save them from the penalty of sin, and had given them his Spirit to counter the lusts of the flesh and the pride of life (Romans 8:5–11), enabling them to live a life worthy (i.e. befitting, suitable to) the calling they had received (Ephesians 4:1–3).

Christlikeness in marriage

One of the most important areas of life into which all this must be translated is Christian marriage. In his letter to the Ephesians the apostle Paul writes:

> Submit to one another out of reverence for Christ.
> Wives, submit yourselves to your own husbands as you do to the Lord. For the husband is the head of the wife as Christ is the head of the church, his body, of which he is the Saviour.

Now as the church submits to Christ, so also wives should submit to their husbands in everything.

Husbands, love your wives, just as Christ loved the church and gave himself up for her to make her holy, cleansing her by the washing with water through the word, and to present her to himself as a radiant church, without stain or wrinkle or any other blemish, but holy and blameless. In this same way, husbands ought to love their wives as their own bodies. He who loves his wife loves himself.

(Ephesians 5:21–28)

Paul tells the Ephesian believers that wives were to respect their husbands as representing the authority of Christ in their homes; husbands in turn were to love their wives as Christ loved the church and gave himself for her. This was not hierarchy or patriarchy. There was to be a headship without domination, diversity of roles with mutual submission, and partnership without compulsion. Such teaching reflects the privilege of an ordered relationship, not the power of rule; it commends submission, not servitude.

Paul speaks of a voluntary submission, not a forced one. If a wife is asked to submit, it is to her husband's love, not to his tyranny. 'Wives, submit to your husbands *as is fitting in the Lord*' is a qualification that 'recasts the wife's submission to her husband by turning it into allegiance shown to Christ'.[5]

The greatest challenge here is not to the wife, but to the husband, who is told to love his wife as Christ loved the church and gave himself up for her (Ephesians 5:25). This gives marriage a uniquely exalted place and character, not only in principle, but in practice too. Christlikeness in a husband will show itself in very clear and practical ways. As Christ cherishes the church, so husbands are to cherish their wives: protecting and affirming them, recognizing their gifts and developing their potential, celebrating a unique relationship and treating them as one with themselves.

This kind of head loves his wife as his own body, and wants her to flourish and be fulfilled, for in marriage as God created it, 'the two will become one flesh' (Genesis 2:24; Matthew 19:5–6; Ephesians 5:31). In *Mere Christianity* C. S. Lewis famously said:

> The Christian idea of marriage is based on Christ's words that a man and his wife are to be regarded as a single organism – for that is what 'one flesh' would be in modern English. And the Christians believe that when He said this, He was not expressing a sentiment but stating a fact – just as one is stating a fact when one says that a lock and its key are one mechanism, or that a violin and its bow are one instrument.[6]

. . . until Christ is formed in you

True scriptural holiness is broad and balanced, wholesome and human. The Holy Spirit is not only concerned with our quiet times and our church involvement, central though these are in the Christian life, but he goes out with us to our work, making us better students and teachers, better employees and employers, enabling us to contribute to our society and our world by our profession, skill, craft and service.

The apostle Paul expresses concern that the Galatian Christians are in danger of being influenced by false teaching. It is threatening their development, stunting their growth, and even putting their souls in peril. After warning and teaching and encouraging them, he writes to them as, 'My dear children, for whom I am again in the pains of childbirth until Christ is formed in you' (Galatians 4:19). The word he uses there was a term used medically for the forming of an embryo in the womb. 'He is not satisfied that Christ *dwells* in them; he longs to see Christ *formed* in them, to see them transformed into the image of Christ, "until you take the shape of Christ" [NEB].'7

If Christ is to be formed in us, it will be the work of a lifetime, and for that we need more and more of the Holy Spirit's power and help. We need to be daily aware of our dependence on him and his willingness to deepen the likeness of Christ in us in all we do and are.

You and I are constantly made aware of our sinfulness and weakness, but so is the Holy Spirit who continually dwells within us. He does not come and go – he is here to stay. And he is not discouraged, because he knows the goal to which he is working and the end which is assured: a new heavens and earth populated by a people who are like Christ, including you and me. We must continually remind ourselves of this and work from it with determination and hope: 'do not grieve the Holy Spirit of God, with whom you were sealed for the day of redemption' (Ephesians 4:30).

8

The Word of God

The Torah child

Elie Wiesel is a Hungarian-born Jewish-American writer, professor, political activist, Nobel Laureate and Holocaust survivor. He is the author of many books, including *Night*, a work based on his experiences as a prisoner in the Auschwitz, Buna and Buchenwald concentration camps. Victor Shepherd relates this deeply moving story from the Auschwitz period of Wiesel's life, from one of the Nazis' most notorious extermination camps, in 1945:

> Jewish inmates only days away from murder by gassing, their remains then to be burnt in huge crematoria, are praying. Needless to say they had no Scriptures, no Torah scroll. [The Torah scroll is the holiest book of the Jewish scriptures. It contains the first five books of the Bible, the five books of Moses.] What are they going to do at that part of Jewish worship when a Torah scroll is carried around the synagogue sanctuary and worshipers reach out to touch it as it is borne past them?

Elie Wiesel, himself a prisoner in Auschwitz and only fifteen years old at the time, survived to tell us what happened next. Lacking a Torah scroll (these scrolls are about four feet long), someone picked up a little boy, about four feet long, and carried *him* around the prison-barracks so that devout people could reach out and touch him. After all, wasn't Torah to be embodied in a child at any time? Wasn't Torah to be written on human hearts in all circumstances? And so a little boy was carried around the room while older worshipers touched him, the living embodiment of Jewish faith, in hope too that the youngster would survive and bespeak the faith of Abraham and Sarah, Isaac and Rebecca, Jacob and Rachel.

When I first read Wiesel's description of this haunting moment, I thought immediately of the prophet Zechariah and his Spirit-inflamed cry, 'Thus says the Lord of hosts: In those days ten men from the nations of every tongue shall take hold of the robe of a Jew saying, "Let us go with you, for we have heard that God is with you"' [Zechariah 8:22]. The Jews in Auschwitz touched the prison rags of a boy.[1]

The Jews have always been a people of the Book, and they have certainly been a central part of its story. Christians, and indeed a great part of the world, owe an incalculable debt to those who preserved the Scriptures through centuries of national faith and failure, war and deportation. But the supreme revelation of those Scriptures, and the apex of their history as the people to whom God committed the revelation of himself, was to be found in Jesus of Nazareth. And millions have laid hold on that one Jew who said, 'I, when I am lifted up from the earth, will draw all people to myself' (John 12:32). Not a little boy, but the Son of God lifted up.

Jesus and the Old Testament Scriptures

Jesus, the man of prayer, the man filled with the Holy Spirit, was also the man of Scripture. The authority of the Scriptures was the authority of God (Matthew 5:17–18). When Satan sought to deflect him from his true mission, our Lord quoted Scripture to defeat him, replying to each of the temptations, 'It is written . . . It is written . . . It is written' (Matthew 4:4, 7, 10).

As we saw in chapter 1, Jesus lived his life deeply aware of the prophecies about him. He rebuked his critics in Jerusalem with the words: 'You study the Scriptures diligently because you think that in them you have eternal life. These are the very Scriptures that testify about me, yet you refuse to come to me to have life' (John 5:39–40). As they approached Jerusalem for the last time, Jesus took the Twelve aside and told them:

> We are going up to Jerusalem, and everything that is written by the prophets about the Son of Man will be fulfilled. He will be handed over to the Gentiles. They will mock him, insult him and spit on him; they will flog him and kill him. On the third day he will rise again.
> (Luke 18:31–33)

Jesus himself remained in control of the events surrounding his death, consciously fulfilling Scripture (John 10:18; 13:26–27), and on the cross at his death it was the Scriptures that were uppermost in his mind. His prayer, 'Father, forgive them, for they do not know what they are doing' (Luke 23:34), was probably shaped by the Law, which allowed atonement for sins of ignorance (Leviticus 5:17–19; Numbers 15:25–31).

His experience of abandonment by God as he took our place, bearing our sin and its punishment, was expressed in the words of Psalm 22: 'My God, my God, why have you forsaken me?' (verse 1), and his statement: 'I am thirsty' (John 19:28) echoes the psalmist's experience in the same psalm (verse 15). That psalm ends with triumph and the assurance that future generations will share in it. As Derek Kidner points out, 'The psalm which began with the cry of dereliction ends with the word "he has wrought it", an announcement not far removed from our Lord's great cry, "It is finished" [accomplished].'[2]

After his death and resurrection we find Jesus, not making a public display of his new resurrection life, but giving seminars to his wondering disciples on Old Testament prophecies about himself: 'And beginning with Moses and all the Prophets, he explained to them what was said in all the Scriptures concerning himself' (Luke 24:27, 45–48).

If we want to be Christlike, then we too must give Scripture the priority in our lives that he gave it in his. Then we shall find that it speaks to us as it spoke to him, and that as it gives him a unique place as God's Son, so too it will give us our place in God's plan as the people of his Redeemer-Son.

Jesus and the New Testament Scriptures

Before his departure, Jesus promised that he would send the Holy Spirit to equip the disciples to be the foundational teachers of the church, enabling them to remember his teaching and understand the meaning of his death and resurrection. He validated the inspiration and teaching of the New Testament in advance when he told the disciples soon to become his apostles and the leaders of the new church:

I have much more to say to you, more than you can now bear. But when he, the Spirit of truth, comes, he will guide you into all the truth. He will not speak on his own; he will speak only what he hears, and he will tell you what is yet to come. He will glorify me because it is from me that he will receive what he will make known to you. All that belongs to the Father is mine. That is why I said the Spirit will receive from me what he will make known to you.

(John 16:12–15)

That is why we must never put the rest of the New Testament on a lower level than the Gospels. Jesus is *continuing* to teach by his Holy Spirit through the apostles. And without the apostolic teaching about Jesus and his saving work, we would have no Christianity.

Imagine a film of the life of Jesus, but without any sound. There you see a baby laid in a manger, a man being immersed in water, then speaking to crowds, and finally on a cross, and an empty tomb. What are you to make of it? It is a silent movie, all very enigmatic and uncertain.

But when the sound is turned up, everything becomes coherent and clear. The 'soundtrack' of the gospel events is the apostles' teaching: the apostolic explanation of the birth of Jesus as the incarnation of God, the death of Jesus as a sin-bearing sacrifice, the resurrection of Jesus as the sign of his success, and the spread of the church as the growth of the kingdom of God leading on to his Second Coming. And this is not merely a commentary: the apostolic proclamation of the Christ-event is part of the Christ-event, Christ speaking to the churches by his Spirit.

God's Word for today – and every day!

In the New Testament the earlier Old Testament Scriptures are not made irrelevant by the coming of Jesus. Shortly before his death, the apostle Paul wrote to his younger colleague Timothy, warning him of the pressures to conform to an increasingly godless society:

> But as for you, continue in what you have learned and have become convinced of, because you know those from whom you learned it, and how from infancy you have known the Holy Scriptures, which are able to make you wise for salvation through faith in Christ Jesus.
>
> (2 Timothy 3:14–15)

Timothy had been brought up to know the truth, beauty and power of the Scriptures, and he had learned from Paul's first preaching in his home town of Lystra (Acts 16:1–5) that Jesus Christ was the goal to which they all led. Verses 16 and 17 of 2 Timothy, chapter 3, offer an outstanding statement: 'All Scripture is God-breathed and is useful for teaching, rebuking, correcting and training in righteousness, so that the servant of God may be thoroughly equipped for every good work.'

And God who is in the Scriptures is also in the reader! Why does the Bible have such persisting power with God's people? Because, first and foremost, its Author is the Holy Spirit who inspired it and who accompanies it into the hearts and lives of God's people. That is why, when we feel outnumbered and discouraged, and the Bible is dismissed as out of date and unbelievable, we should be undaunted in our reverence of the Scriptures, since only those who have the Spirit of God can properly comprehend and embrace God's Word.

Its first power is positive: to make us in love with God, to show us the beauty of the life that pleases God, and to draw us into that life. This is the life that we see in his Son, Jesus, a life that has touched us and changed us, and is changing us still, deepening in us that Christlikeness which pleases the

Father and witnesses to the world (John 17:6–8, 17–19, 20–26). If the Holy Spirit is the supreme *agent* of our sanctification, then the Bible is the chief *instrument* of our sanctification.

So we must read our Bible for three things: understanding, experience and direction. We will look at all three below.

Reading for understanding

The first is crucial: *understanding*. Jesus 'opened their minds so they could understand the Scriptures' (Luke 24:45). The Bible seeks to change our thinking before it seeks to change our behaviour. It does not call for blind obedience, and it does not keep us at nursery level. For his followers, Jesus prayed, 'Sanctify them by the truth; your word is truth' (John 17:17). The key to maturity, according to Paul, is a right understanding of your life in Christ. The frequency with which he refers to *the mind* in this and other regards is striking.

As theologian Robert Banks makes plain, Paul says that growth takes place within the communities of the church as their members increase in knowledge and are enriched by it, and as they are renewed through knowledge and filled with it (1 Corinthians 1:5; Colossians 1:9–10; 3:10). Elsewhere Paul speaks of growth coming via 'the renewing of [their] mind' (Romans 12:2), and it is on this basis that he urges them to 'set [their] minds on things above' (Colossians 3:2) and to be 'like-minded' in their understanding of the things of God and its outworking (Philippians 2:1–2).[3]

Reading for experience

The second too is crucial: we read the Word of God for an *experience* of God. This is not only an emotional thing. When we read, we should pray for the *impact* of the passage, and not just read it as students learning academically. Remember to ask God to make it a word to you personally, and pray,

'Let me hear your voice and see your face as I read your Word.' There is a power in the Word of God, which comes from the Holy Spirit who first inspired it, and it is a power which the Holy Spirit releases as we read and seek God. It is not given automatically or evenly, but given as we seek persistently and humbly. And it is given in different ways at different times.

We need the perspective God's Word brings to our lives and the lives of those around us. We need the light it shines on dubious practices and hollow boasts. We need the commanding voice with which it speaks, and sometimes shouts, when our feet are slipping and temptation is strong. We need its confirmations and its consolations. We need it in youth and in old age, on life's peaks and in its troughs, and at its end.

Reading for direction

The third thing we look for is crucial also: we are to read the Word of God for *direction* in life at all its levels. Christlikeness comes with obedience, and obedience waits for direction. The ancient Jewish word *Torah* did not merely mean 'law' in the sense of legislation, but was a much broader term, including counsel and direction (Psalm 119:1–8; Proverbs 1:1–7). When we read the Word of God, we must ask ourselves, 'What must I *do* with this? What difference does God want to make in my life, my relationships and my career? And above all, how can I worship God through this passage? Am I prepared for the challenges as well as the comforts?' With biblical thinking, we need to demonstrate biblical living, both private and public.

An Old Testament psalmist put it this way: 'I have hidden your word in my heart that I might not sin against you' (Psalm 119:11). That is its tendency and effect when the Spirit who inspired it changes our hearts to revere it.

When John Wesley left home, his mother, Susannah, is said to have written these words on the flyleaf of his Bible: 'Sin will keep you from this book, but this book will keep you from sin.'

The traveller and the tripper

One of the most pressing needs among Christian believers today is to become better acquainted with the Bible. We need to read it systematically, alternating Old and New Testaments. Take time to read parts of the Bible that are less familiar to you. Become aware of the many popular helps and commentaries available through publishers like IVP. These will give background and body to the text. Some Bible study helps are very short daily readings; some offer an in-depth commentary on a particular book, giving the background and meaning of each chapter. One of the older guides posed a series of questions after each passage of Scripture, many of them calling for both self-examination and action. Indeed, should we not always let the Bible question us as we read? Find the level that is right for you and determine to study God's Word in all its truth and relevance for every age and every generation. Don't just 'dip', looking for an attractive verse or two.

Donald Barnhouse was an American preacher well known for his illustrations. Speaking on the need for serious study of the Bible, he said:

> The author of a celebrated travel-book on Italy once remarked that in his youth Italy had been the land of the traveller but it had become the land of the tripper. 'They don't understand what they see' he lamented. One girl who had 'travelled' in Italy said she remembered Rome as the place where the shoe-polish spilled on her best dress, and Venice as the place where the hairdresser burned her hair with curling irons.[4]

Barnhouse asks the question: 'Have you really spent time with the Word of God, or are you a tripper?'

The Bible in our churches

In our churches too the place of Scripture should be paramount, allowing God to speak through our Sunday readings and teaching, and with our preachers and teachers reinforcing and applying what it says to us all. Those who speak should show every evidence of having studied the passage closely in both its immediate and its wider context in Scripture, and should apply it thoughtfully from a pastoral perspective and the wider world scene. It is by such means that the people of God have been strong in faith and kept true to God in life. Paul writes to Timothy with the urgency and priorities of a mentor who will not be there for him much longer:

> In the presence of God and of Christ Jesus, who will judge
> the living and the dead, and in view of his appearing and his
> kingdom, I give you this charge: preach the word; be prepared
> in season and out of season; correct, rebuke and encourage –
> with great patience and careful instruction.
> (2 Timothy 4:1–2)

The Holy Spirit (chapter 7) loves to work with Holy Scripture (chapter 8) since he himself first gave it, and by it he works not only in the individual's heart but in the community of believers. As the Word of God is taught and preached in the churches, as its message is received and sung by congregations, as it is discussed and applied in groups, so Paul's words to the Colossians are fulfilled:

Let the message of Christ dwell among you richly as you teach and admonish one another with all wisdom through psalms, hymns and songs from the Spirit, singing to God with gratitude in your hearts.

(Colossians 3:16)

9

The place of prayer

It must have been a strange sight – a blind boy flying a kite with his father's help. A friend of the family who was watching dared to ask him a question: 'What do you get out of this when you can't see the kite?' The answer was simple enough. The boy replied, 'I can't see it, but I can feel the pull.'

Christians might make a similar reply to the questions: 'Why pray to a God you can't see? Why put so much effort into an exercise that is so unquantifiable?' The answer might well be: 'I can't see what's happening, but I can feel the pull.'

We pray for many reasons, but first and foremost because God commands it. God puts meaning into life and would not call us to a meaningless task. Second, we pray because God is glorified in it: his presence is everywhere so that he hears us, his perfect knowledge so that he knows our thoughts and hearts, his goodness and grace so that we are encouraged to come to him even in our sin and need. And we pray because we ourselves are changed by it – as we pray we grow: changes occur in minds and hearts and lives. We often find too that situations beyond our power are changed as we continue to pray, and sometimes the answers to prayer are dramatic.

Coincidence?

One of the most dramatic answers to prayer was given to a church I know in Dunstable. A series of brutal attacks and rapes had been carried out in the area by a criminal known in the popular press as 'the Fox' because of his skill in evading the police. It became national news in a big way.

Eventually a local church held special prayer meetings for the capture of the criminal. They prayed specifically, forcefully and persistently. Soon afterwards 'the Fox' was captured, and a picture of the criminal appeared in the newspapers, handcuffed between two policemen.

Someone might say that it was inevitable that he would be captured sometime, and that it was a coincidence, not cause (prayer) and effect (capture). But how does it look if I tell you that both of the policemen in the photograph were members of that praying church? Was that God's comment on 'coincidence'?

The praying Christ

There is no greater encouragement to a life of prayer than the life and teaching of Jesus. Did he need to pray? Then surely we need to do so too. His prayer life focused his sense of dependence and obedience. He depended on God his Father and did nothing without his Spirit's guidance.

It was as he was praying at his baptism that heaven was opened, the Spirit descended like a dove and the voice of his Father spoke, 'You are my Son, whom I love; with you I am well pleased' (Luke 3:22). Jesus spent an entire night in prayer before choosing the twelve disciples from the many who followed him (Luke 6:12–16). He prayed in the quiet of retreats (Luke 9:18, 28) and in the strenuous demands of his public ministry (Matthew 14:23). He told his followers to pray and taught them how to do so (Matthew 6:5–13), and he prayed for them and for us (John 17:9, 11, 15, 20). At the climax of his life he prayed in Gethsemane (Matthew 26:36–46), and even on the cross he prayed for those crucifying him (Luke 23:34). The testimony of Scripture is that he prayed then and he prays now. In heaven he is still the praying Christ (Hebrews 7:25).

Eye contact with God

The foremost characteristic of Jesus' prayer life was the relationship that he had with God: unique and intimate, dependent and confident. This is the first lesson for us too. Above all else we must be mindful that our relationship with God is a *personal* one. The metaphors of Scripture include God as parent, husband, lover and friend, and Eugene Peterson insists, 'God is not someone or something to be talked *about* . . . God is not an idea to be studied . . . God is not a problem to be solved.' God is 'a *thou* to whom we speak, not an *it* that we talk about. Prayer is the attention we give to the One who attends to us.'[1]

Prayer has been called 'eye contact with God'. In Scripture it is called 'seeking the face of God'. And the important thing is to know that in such seeking there is finding, for God is not waiting at the end of our prayers – he is there at the start too. He is in the seeking as well as the finding: encouraging our prayers and helping them, accepting them and willing to be honoured by them. He is as ready to be as pleased with our approaches as any parent is with a child. Often attributed to

Bernard of Clairvaux is the wonderful prayer: 'I never come to You but by You; I never go from You without You.' There are few things that challenge and humble us as our efforts to pray do. They are so often crossed with wandering thoughts, weakened with tiredness and cooled by neglected disciplines, that we are tempted to think they can do no good, and that God thinks as little of them as we do. Yet the most wonderful thing about prayer is that God has provided for all our inadequacies: there is grace to cover all our prayers as well as all our sins.

And what is the role of the Trinity in prayer?

The Three who listen to us

Christians believe that God is the Father, the Son and the Holy Spirit: the three persons of the Holy Trinity. And in prayer we are always in conversation with the Three; they hear us, help us and surround us with their blessing. I pray, marvelling at my heavenly Father who has loved and chosen me, kneeling before the Son who died for my sin and rose for my justification, and opening my deepest heart to the Holy Spirit who with amazing patience and love is making me holy too.

When we worship One, we are including All. John Calvin wrote, 'That passage of Gregory of Nazianzus vastly delights me: "I cannot think on the one without quickly being encircled by the splendour of the three; nor can I discern the three without being straightway carried back to the one." '[2]

The Three who work for us

The teaching of the New Testament is that whenever we pray, we should be aware that we have a listening Father, a praying Christ in heaven and a praying Holy Spirit on earth. Jesus said that God is our heavenly Father who always hears us even when we pray alone and in secret, who calls us to pray even though he knows our needs before we ask him, and who loves to hear our voice in prayer (Matthew 6:6–8). In the letter to the Hebrews we learn that the Christ who prayed for us on earth (John 17:20) still prays for us in heaven (Hebrews 4:14–16; 7:25). And in Paul's letter to the Romans we are told that as the Lord Jesus is praying for us in heaven, the Holy Spirit is praying for us on earth, praying in our hearts, praying in our prayers, inspiring our longings with his own desires (Romans 8:26–27).

The Three who call us to join them

So there is this great river of prayer flowing between the persons of the Trinity: the Father, the Son and the Holy Spirit. And our prayers are being taken up into it, joined with it and flowing with it in its mighty current. Is that not a staggering thought? Through all eternity Father, Son and Holy Spirit have had communion, fellowship and joyful interaction. The tremendous testimony of God's Word is this: that *we* are taken up in the divine work; *we* become part of the eternal conversation; *our* prayers are used to fulfil the sovereign plan.

When you realize this and take it deeply into your prayer life, then however small a part your prayers may form of the heavenly intercession of Christ or the mighty movement of the Holy Spirit in his ministry of prayer on earth, they are hugely significant and truly effective. Pray with the praying Spirit. Pray with the praying Christ. Pray to the loving Father. Prayer cannot fail when it is according to the will of God, because it is part of this bigger picture and this greater power.

Yet it's not always easy. Why?

Christlike in persistent prayer

Jesus urged his followers to, 'Ask . . . seek . . . knock' and 'it *will* be given to you . . . you *will* find . . . the door *will* be opened to you' (see Matthew 7:7). We need such reassurance in the face of an unbelieving world and many setbacks. In the parable of the persistent widow (Luke 18:1–8) Jesus tells the story of a woman's forlorn cause. She seems to have no chance in a man's world, without a protector or an advocate, and with a stronger, noisier crowd shouldering its way to the front and an unjust judge in power who doesn't care. Yet, by her persistence and the judge's fear of dishonour, her cause triumphs.

What chance does the kingdom of God have in a world of unjust judges, where love, humility, meekness and forgiveness seem defenceless against pride, selfishness and greed? But into just such a world Christ Jesus has brought the beginnings of God's future kingdom, the only one that will last for ever. There would be opposition and setbacks. It would be scorned, hated, opposed and threatened. And it always will be too until God comes to judge the world in righteousness in one final act.

Meanwhile there are to be two great forces of prayer in a world of injustice and suffering and rebellion against God: the prayers of Christ in heaven and the prayers of God's people on earth. So Jesus told his disciples a parable to show them that 'they should always pray and not give up' (Luke 18:1).

Reasons for delay

Why does God not answer prayer immediately? He has the power, he has the will, and he has the goodness, so why do we have to work through opposition, delay and unbelief?

Perhaps because God himself has to work through opposition, delay and unbelief. Perhaps he is reminding us that we are dealing with people who need to be persuaded, not puppets who simply need a different string pulled. Perhaps he is calling us to be partners with him in his wisdom, patience, persistence and love. Perhaps too he is showing us that we are fighting a long battle with eternal consequences, and building a kingdom which is here to last. That takes time. A cardboard kingdom could be put up in no time, but an eternal kingdom takes rather longer!

God's work in people is not easily done; we are not puppets, we are moral agents. *Prayer* takes time to work, because *God* takes time to work – in all of us. He has to work against much ignorance and many prejudices, against fears, inconsistencies and follies. God is rejected every day, so why should we complain if we are rejected every day? Yet God comes back every day with persistent mercy, so why should we not come back every day with persistent prayer? God's persistence only wins through after many rebuffs, and he calls us to share in that work.

Battlefield prayer

In teaching on this subject we often hear the term 'petitionary prayer'. A petition is a solemn supplication or request, especially to a superior authority, often made by many people. Petitionary prayer involves thoughtful deliberate prayer requests, often about the wider scene in our fallen world, about matters far from home or beyond our own power to change. In it the persistent cry of the church, against the unbelief and despair, the sorrow and suffering, the hatred and spiritual darkness of our fallen world, is 'Your kingdom come!'

'What is the nature of petitionary prayer?' asks David Wells, in a major book on world mission. He answers his own question:

It is in essence rebellion – rebellion against the world in its fallenness, the absolute and undying refusal to accept as normal what is pervasively abnormal . . . Petitionary prayer only flourishes where there is a two-fold belief: first, that God's name is hallowed too irregularly, his kingdom has come too little, and his will is done too infrequently; second that God himself can change this situation.[3]

Prayer becomes rebellion against the rebellion of earth. It fights for God and it knows that it is fighting on the winning side.

Popular author John Piper uses a favourite metaphor in *Let the Nations Be Glad*, his book on world mission:

Life is war . . . prayer is primarily a wartime walkie-talkie for the mission of the church as it advances against the powers of darkness and unbelief. It is not surprising that prayer malfunctions when we try to make it a domestic walkie-talkie . . . Prayer gives us the significance of front-line forces, and gives God the glory of a limitless Provider. The one who gives the power gets the glory. Thus prayer safeguards the supremacy of God in missions while linking us with endless grace for every need.[4]

Paul reminds us that it is prayer which puts on the whole armour of God (Ephesians 6:10–18), and he himself is so aware of its potency even in the hands of the weakest that he asks for prayer to continue and complete his own ministry (6:19–20) – even though he is in chains for the gospel. This is not a war without wounds, and the persecuted church should never be far from our own prayers and the public prayers of our churches. We must join our voices with those suffering Christians around the world who are surrounded by hostility and penalized by discrimination.

God and one man's prayers

We noted earlier that Jesus preached the parable of the persistent widow to show his followers that 'they should always pray and not give up' (Luke 18:1), a consistent part of his teaching on prayer (Matthew 7:7–8; Luke 11:9–13). The most memorable demonstration of such prayer that I have heard of occurred some years back with two people I have known well.

One of our church members is Elsie Harris. Elsie and her husband John (now in heaven with the Lord) worked for the Leprosy Mission for forty years, mostly in Nepal and Congo (as it was known then).

A few years ago Elsie received a letter, relating to a time about thirty-five years earlier in their career. To understand the context, you need to know that John and Elsie had a very profound and sustained intercessory prayer ministry, of which John spoke very little, which reached into every day (and night) of their lives.

In 1969 they were living and working in the Kathmandu Valley, about twenty miles from Kathmandu itself. In those days no one was allowed to witness to Christ to the Nepalese. Ex-pats in the hospital could have their own church services, but there was to be no evangelism whatsoever. It was a closed country.

During their work, John and Elsie had become increasingly concerned about the nearby Lille Valley. For all its natural beauty, it was then a place of such spiritual darkness and occult power that the missionaries used to say this could be felt by Christians who passed near.

One day a mother brought a child to the leprosy hospital for some attention, though neither had leprosy. This child was very dirty and scruffy, and as John was talking with the mother and the child, he felt a tremendous conviction that this ten-year-old would be used to open up the notorious Lille Valley to the gospel.

It seemed a ridiculous thing, but John felt the assurance of the Holy Spirit that it would certainly happen, so he covenanted with God to pray every day for the child and this outcome. He prayed for seventeen years, every day without fail, even when the Harrises left Nepal to take up leprosy work in Congo.

In 1986, when visiting Nepal, they heard from a paramedic friend named James that the Lille Valley had indeed opened up to the gospel. Soon afterwards, James wrote with details that entire families had become Christians through the witness of one woman. John asked simply, 'What is the name of this woman?' 'Daya,' his friend said – and Daya was the very person John had treated so many years before!

Not long after John died, Daya wrote to Elsie to say that James, the paramedic, had told her that it was John who had treated her as a girl and prayed for her down through the years. Neither she nor her mother had ever known of John's conviction, but she was writing to Elsie to say that there were now whole groups of worshippers in the Lille Valley.

Later Elsie received another letter from her to say that they were standing strong in the faith of Jesus Christ. They had opened a tearoom, and there is now even a plaque to John Harris in open celebration of the gospel of Jesus Christ. A small church has been formed where before only idol worship was allowed.

That, it seems to me, is a modern example of what we read in the Acts of the Apostles: the power of the Spirit at work in a deeply spiritual person, God sharing his secrets with a praying man and taking him into partnership, and God doing mighty things through believing prayer. But remember, this was a case of a *given* assurance, a prophetic revelation of God's Spirit, and it was given to a man of prayer. God does not tell his secrets to those who only drop in for a chat.

10

The people of God

Right train, wrong carriage

Years ago I was due to speak to a group of evangelists and other leaders. After a demanding week and a very early start, I was not in the sunniest frame of mind as I stood on a cold platform, well before dawn, waiting for the early train. When it did come, I was glad to find an empty rear carriage where I could at least read.

As the train began its journey, I pulled out a book and opened it – but suddenly realized that the lights weren't on and I couldn't read the print. Now me without a book is a sorry sight, but worse was to come. The compartment was freezing, and I realized that the heating wasn't on either. Having paid in full for my ticket, I thought I was being short-changed. Feeling increasingly irritated, I mused on what I was going to say to the ticket collector. But no such person came, and I remained alone, cold and in the dark.

Eventually I decided to walk the length of the train to find an employee and register my complaint. I strode through the dark and the cold, composing my little speech as the train swayed. (Now, I don't usually complain, but when I do, I do it properly.) Soon I saw a crack of light and thought, 'Ah, the driver/inspector/collector, cosy in their front cab, I expect.' I pulled open the connecting door, and saw to my astonishment the usual collection of early-morning travellers, snug and warm and no doubt quite good-tempered and feeling content with British Rail.

Immediately the ticket collector materialized and apologetically explained that the electrics had failed in the rear carriages, but only in those. The rest of the train was as it should be, and would I like to take a seat in the warm and the light? I was just sitting in the wrong carriage!

This might be the picture of many Christians' experience and that of many churches too. There are Christians who, as it were, are in the right train, but the wrong carriage. They are undeniably saved because of what Christ has done for them: they too have been loved from eternity, separated for God, and have a place in his church among his people. But there is something wrong with the electrics: their Christian lives lack warmth and light; they are not, to be sure, entirely in the dark, but their lives are not burning brightly in a world that is indeed in the dark.

There are churches too where worship is correct but formal, the life of faith is shared but distant, understanding, like the teaching given, is too limited, and there is pettiness and division and the faith of infants has not grown up (1 Corinthians 3:1). The church is then a cold carriage. But it doesn't have to be like this, and there is a better way for us all.

We all need churches.

Christlike together

When the Lord Jesus calls his people, he also gathers them into churches. Churches are the expression of God's own life in the trinitarian community of Father, Son and Holy Spirit; human beings are made in God's image in their social life, not just their solitary life.

The full image of God in human beings, in its wisdom, power and beauty, is not found in any one of us alone, but in all of us in relationship. There was only ever one man who had it all – and even he sought company and called disciples and turned every feast into a foretaste of the messianic banquet in the age to come. Not much trace of isolationism there!

And so he invented the church – that is to say, he planned churches, for we should not speak of the church without thinking of churches, lest we get too theoretical and mystical. In Paul's letters to the Corinthians, Galatians and Thessalonians the word 'church' always means the local church. In Ephesians and Colossians Paul uses it of the universal church, in heaven and on earth, past, present and future, the church in its completeness as it is in the mind of God. Everywhere in the New Testament the local, gathered, even structured, church is prominent, and the picture used to define it is that of a body, not a force field, with gifts and leadership, discipline and purpose, consolation and encouragement.

Some people like to think you can be just as good a Christian outside churches as inside them. But that is hardly true. It may be that *some* believers, wonderfully good, might be better off without *some* churches, disgracefully bad, but most people and most churches find themselves somewhere in the middle.

Living in relationship

It is a feature of our humanity that we find our true identity and our real purpose in living in relationship with God and other people. In church we find our place as members of the family of God, the body of Christ, the kingdom he is building for eternity. We find encouragement and affirmation in its Sunday gatherings and weekly home groups.

When you are assailed by unfair treatment at work or misunderstood in the world, you can find relief and appreciation in the community of faith. When you are sick or depressed or old and feeble, then you can read again your identity in God: the prayers of your church for you confirm it, their faith strengthens yours, and their care ministers to you. Week by week, finding yourself among the people of God, you know you have your place in the church of God and remember who you are and that you are not alone. This is God's way of reaching you in human words and with a human touch, reminding you where you belong and that you are his.

The twist in the rope

We need one another in order to be strong. In difficult and doubting times you may well feel that everyone else in the church is as flawed and limited as you are. But like so much else, a church is greater than the sum of its parts. A rope, for example, has greater strength than the combined *individual* strength of the strands that make it up. Why is that? It is quite simple. Individual strands have weak spots along them, points at which they easily break. But in a rope, the weak spots are randomly distributed along the length of the rope, and the twist in the rope allows the surrounding strands to cancel out the weak spots of the individual fibres.

It's the same with people. We all have strengths and weaknesses. On our own, our weaknesses can break us, but together we work to achieve strength for all. There are strengths in the church that can cancel out your own weaknesses and inadequacies, and you have strengths that we need.

Sanctification is social

The church is God's instrument of change in our own lives. The Lord Jesus Christ is maturing and developing us, discipling and sanctifying us, guiding and using us along with other people in the communities that we call churches. The biblical teaching is that godliness is a community project, sanctification is social, and we cannot be holy alone.

Churches are God's plan for his glory and our growth. He is glorified in our church life in ways that he cannot be glorified in our solitary lives, and he is glorified in unique ways in our public worship and corporate life.

We need one another even when we get exasperated with each other, and we are called to each other even when we would rather be called somewhere else. We have a responsibility to, and for, each other – true Christian love does not walk away and let other believers sink or swim.

As we read the New Testament letters, the epistles, we soon find that Paul and Peter and John and James and the writer of Hebrews are all writing to people who belong to churches, not to people as isolated units. Indeed, they insist that these people will not flourish in their Christian lives if they ignore the family of God, the body of Christ in that place, for they will be leading rather selfish and self-enclosed lives.

We live in a time of bloated individualism. We are encouraged to think, 'It's all about me' and my self-development because 'I'm worth it' and 'you deserve it'. But when everyone else is pulling away with the same kind of reasoning about themselves, there can only be less service and more competition, less giving and more taking, less sacrifice and more selfishness. And consequently there can only be more loneliness, more isolation, and finally, disillusionment.

Sin always puts a person at the centre, but eventually leaves them cheated because we are not really at the centre, and when we are out of place, out of our proper order and true orbit, we are like wandering meteorites travelling further and further into the darkness.

The church – the shared life of Christ

The Christian life in the New Testament is a shared life. And grace is a shared thing: it comes from the one (Christ), but through the many (fellow believers). It comes to us through shared joys and shared concerns, through mutual prayer and care, through one another's ministries, gifts and encouragements. Christianity is shared life in Christ: praying, playing, worshipping, witnessing and caring together – young and old, hot and cold, timid and bold. As Calvin says in his commentary on 2 Corinthians 6:17, 'God dwells in the midst by dwelling in each one.' To fail to see this is to miss his presence, provision and even his answer to our prayers.

In his book *The Community of the King*, Howard Snyder says:

> The church's first task is to *be* the redeemed community . . .
> to the extent that the Church grows and expands throughout
> the world and demonstrates true Christian community, to
> that extent the kingdom of God has come on earth.[1]

Working together as a body

In his letter to the Romans, Paul writes:

> For just as each of us has one body with many members, and
> these members do not all have the same function, so in Christ
> we, though many, form one body, and each member belongs

to all the others. We have different gifts, according to the grace given to each of us. If your gift is prophesying, then prophesy in accordance with your faith; if it is serving, then serve; if it is teaching, then teach; if it is to encourage, then give encouragement; if it is giving, then give generously; if it is to lead, do it diligently; if it is to show mercy, do it cheerfully. (Romans 12:4–8)

Notice how these gifts, almost chosen at random from among many others, are all placed on the same level. Here is no proud hierarchy of gifts or gifted individuals. Everyone is valued. Some gifts may be more dramatic than others; some may seem to be less 'supernatural' or even less 'spiritual' than others. But in fact all gifts belong to Christ, all are given by him, and in the hands of the Holy Spirit all the gifts have a supernatural character and a supernatural identity: prophecy and serving, public teaching and private counselling, leading from the platform and tending the sick in the bedroom, sharing wealth and showing mercy.

Everyone has something; no one has everything

Paul sees each local church as a graced and gifted community where everyone has something and no one has everything, where every gift is needed and every gift is treasured. All sorts of things, and not just your things or mine, are to be 'done', but they are to be done, as Paul puts it to the Corinthians, 'in a fitting and orderly way' (1 Corinthians 14:40).

It is all too common to find the few doing the work of the many because there is no one else who is willing and able. It is even the case that some have suffered burn-out while others have sat back and done next to nothing. So the body of Christ is not functioning as it should. This demands of us all a right assessment of our ministries. So much is 'locked up', hidden or even sleeping; so many talents lie buried or unused.

On the other hand, the body must work as a unity or it doesn't properly work at all. If limbs convulse and jerk out of control, we call it 'ataxia' and regard it as a handicap. Similarly, where some gifts are overdeveloped and under-controlled in the local church, we shall have a body suffering from ataxia, thrashing around, breaking the china and not building the church (1 Corinthians 14).

As we saw earlier, the picture of a healthy church in the New Testament is always that of a serving church, a church in unity and harmony and mutual care, 'not looking to your own interests but each of you to the interests of the others' (Philippians 2:4).

Loving is often hard work and calls for dogged persistence. It is the daily business of living, serving and caring:

> This is how we know what love is: Jesus Christ laid down his life for us. And we ought to lay down our lives for our brothers and sisters. If anyone has material possessions and sees a brother or a sister in need but has no pity on them, how can the love of God be in that person?
> (1 John 3:16–17)

We cannot be passengers in the church we attend. Rather, we are called to be workers with Christ.

The travel-sick bus conductor

Many years ago I was travelling by bus up one of the valley corridors in South Wales. It was always a miserable, slow, stop-start journey for me, with the driver crashing through the gears and the bus filling up with fumes. As I tend to get travel-sick on buses, I sat in the front near the door where I could at least breathe some clean air at each stop. A woman came and sat next to me and, as we talked, it became clear that she had the same problem. She said she always felt sick on the bus on Saturdays, her day off, when she went as a passenger to visit her elderly father. Indeed, she often had to get off the bus at the stop before her destination. Then she astonished me by telling me that for many years she had been a bus conductor on that very route!

'How on earth could someone given to travel-sickness be a bus conductor?' I asked. 'Well,' she said, in that confidential way that Welsh people have, 'I don't know how it was, but whenever I was working, going up and down the bus giving out tickets, I was fine. It was only when I was a passenger that I got sick!'

We are not to be passengers in our local church or out of it. As passengers, we easily get travel-sick on the journey to heaven: our doubts grow, we become critical of others, disillusioned with the church, more and more on the edge of church life, and increasingly vulnerable to that old trio of temptation: the world, the flesh and the devil. Jesus calls us to be busy for God: 'My Father is always at his work to this very day, and I too am working' (John 5:17). The time is short: 'As long as it is day, we must do the works of him who sent me. Night is coming, when no one can work' (John 9:4). 'Anyone who chooses to do the will of God will find out whether my teaching comes from God or whether I speak on my own' (John 7:17). The needs are many. And remember, it is not a matter of great talent and splendid achievement. The local church can multiply and increase your single effectiveness a hundred times.

The local church is God's chief agency for the evangelism of any village, town or city. When guests come in and see the new community at worship, they begin to see something of the kingdom and the power and the glory of God that a solitary individual can hardly show. Its people are scattered in their witness to Christ, but concentrated in their demonstration of the change he brings to any society where his lordship is truly and properly honoured, where love and service abound, and where there is no segregation of class or colour or status or race.

Can we take Jesus seriously and his church casually? Can Jesus be central and the church marginal in the same life? Can we be good disciples and bad churchmen and women? The answer of the New Testament is an emphatic 'No'!

Here then are some of the main helps we all have in growing in Christlikeness throughout our Christian lives: the Holy Spirit, God's Word the Bible, prayer every day and the community of faith – the church, both local and worldwide. With such massive assistance available to us every day of our lives, we should never despair or give up. Ever. Even in the face of the contradictions we meet in the world and feel in ourselves. And it is to these we now turn.

Part 4
The contradictions of Christlikeness

11

Facing the contradictions in our society

Three-dimensional people in a two-dimensional world

Years ago a young woman in our church who had been touched by the morning service and sermon said to me, 'Why is it that these things which are so precious on Sunday often feel so distant by Wednesday, and my attempts to explain my faith at work come over as flat and unconvincing?' I replied something like this: 'Don't be surprised, you must remember that you live in a *flat* world!' Many people live two-dimensional lives where God is concerned. He is not allowed to enter with his depth and purpose and meaning. And you have to pray and bear witness, where you can, to the fact that there is more, a great deal more, a whole dimension, which gives value and purpose to every life. You are now a three-dimensional person in a two-dimensional world: God, and a relationship with him, is the third dimension. You have it, and they don't – many do not even believe there is a third dimension. But you must live it out in faith and love, and show its beauty, truth and power.

And in your church life you are helped to do so: in worship, in home groups and in fellowship in this community of three-dimensional people who know the God you know and follow his Son Jesus Christ as Lord and Saviour.

Moving from the Tropics to the Arctic

However, this hostility to God (Romans 8:7) and wilful blindness (Ephesians 4:17–18) takes its toll on the Christian, and at times we can feel very isolated in the workplace and even in the family. Every Christian knows, to some extent, the contrasts involved: the highs and lows, the hopes and fears, the fellowship and the alienation.

We move from life in the church to life in the world outside, from life in the believing community to life in an unbelieving society. On Sunday you are with people for whom God is central. On Monday you are likely to be with people for whom God is marginal. On Sunday you worship with those for whom Jesus Christ is Saviour and Lord and loved. On Monday you may work with someone for whom 'Jesus Christ' is no more than a swear word. On Sunday you are in the Tropics. On Monday you are in the Arctic! People feel very threatened by God, by the thought of standing before him when they die, by the closeness of his approach when Christians speak of him, by his claims to be Lord of their lives. And, frankly, sometimes people react badly, scarcely knowing why. So they lash out. And consequently Christians, true Christians, have always been at risk in society if they speak up for God.

'Leave Jesus out of it'

In John's writings 'the world' is society organized to keep God out of its affairs. It is not the world in relation to its abilities and its excellencies (which are many), but the world in relation to its God, the Giver of every good and perfect gift (James 1:17). While 'the world' often retains its religions and its gods, they are not those of the Bible, but a reflection of the world in its fallenness and its fear, its capacity for bribery and manipulation, its superstition and its self-congratulation. John is clear that the world is opposed to the lordship of this God in his absolute commitment to right-eousness and truth.

This is seen most fatally in its antagonism to Jesus and those who represent him. It is seen in words from John 17 and what has been called the high priestly prayer of our Lord. Jesus is returning to the Father, but he has been teaching his disciples so that their joy in God might be full, in counterbalance to the world's hatred.

> I have given them your word and the world has hated them,
> for they are not of the world any more than I am of the world.
> My prayer is not that you will take them out of the world but
> that you protect them from the evil one.
> (John 17:14–15)

Controversial Christlikeness

'I have given them your word and the world has hated them.' One of the most unpopular things the Christian believer can say to anyone today is: 'I have the truth'; 'This is the truth'; 'This is true for you as well as for me; it is true for everyone.' People react in anger, and even disgust, at such claims. And this is an acceptable hatred in our society.

But Jesus says he has given us God's Word, and we must be united in loyalty to it. He has also said that he himself is God's Word, God's final Word to the world in its great need of salvation. This is at the same time our danger and our protection, our duty and our joy. We must take that Word out to our generation, first because it is true, and second because there will be those who hear it and believe, receiving this Christ as their peace with God. So Jesus sends us out into a hostile world where we too shall experience the hostility and even persecution that he encountered (John 15:18–25). As Don Carson puts it, 'The followers of Jesus are permitted neither the luxury of compromise . . . nor the safety of disengagement.'[1]

Many of us in the easy, liberal and prosperous West lead a cushioned existence, but we would find that the world around us would not be so liberal if we spoke out more clearly, more boldly and more urgently about sin, righteousness and judgment.

Let's turn now to the role of the Holy Spirit in all of this.

Jesus and the Spirit's witness in the world

But very truly I tell you, it is for your good that I am going away. Unless I go away, the Advocate will not come to you; but if I go, I will send him to you. When he comes, he will prove the world to be in the wrong about sin and righteousness and judgment: about sin, because people do not believe in me; about righteousness, because I am going to the Father, where you can see me no longer; and about judgment, because the prince of this world now stands condemned.
(John 16:7–11)

This is truth for tough times! The Holy Spirit brings three charges to the unbeliever, relating to 'sin, righteousness and judgment'. Here they are so linked with Jesus that it becomes clear that a person's standing before God, and their entire future, depends on their relationship with Jesus Christ as Saviour and Lord.

The first charge is the refusal to repent of the enormous crime of rejecting the Son of God: 'He will prove the world to be in the wrong about sin . . . because people do not believe in me.' The coming of Jesus Christ is the primary fact of world history, yet most who hear of it ignore or resist it, or set it aside for consideration at a more convenient time. These are all forms of the primary sin in human life, one that underlies all other sins: unbelief.

The Holy Spirit accompanies a witnessing people to offer forgiveness and to warn of judgment, to save the church and convict the world. And you and I are among them (John 20:21; Acts 8:4; 2 Corinthians 5:20; 1 Thessalonians 1:8).

The second charge deepens the first. Jesus says of the Spirit, 'He will prove the world to be in the wrong . . . about righteousness, because I am going to the Father.' Here at last is one whom we can trust utterly. Here is truth in the world of half-truth and lies, and here is the way to God in a world of confusion and dead ends (Acts 17:30–31; 2 Corinthians 4:3–6; 10:4–5). Both Jesus and his followers have been vindicated by his resurrection and elevation to God's right hand as Lord of history and Saviour of the world. Jesus' influence and life-changing power have persisted through history and are evident in millions of lives today. The question now is not about Jesus, but about those faced with his claims and offered his salvation: what will they do with it (2 Corinthians 2:14–16)?

The third charge also relates to the devil, the prince of this world: '[The Spirit] will prove the world to be in the wrong . . . about judgment, because the prince of this world now stands condemned.'

Deep inside the human conscience there is the uncomfortable thought that one day that person must give an account of their life to God, a thought that most people run away from or pacify with false reassurances (Acts 24:25; Romans 1:18). That is because the human mind has been darkened with regard to God by Satan the great liar. Now, as ever, he blinds the minds of unbelievers to keep them from seeing 'the light of the gospel that displays the glory of Christ, who is the image of God' (2 Corinthians 4:4), but Jesus says his grip on the nations is about to be challenged and his power will finally be destroyed at the Last Judgment (Luke 10:17–20; John 12:31). Those who follow the god of this world will share his end.

The apostle John warns of the world and its hostility to God (1 John 2:15–17), but firmly traces that hostility to the devil, who deceives, seduces and manipulates people and cultures:

> We know that we are children of God, and that the whole world is under the control of the evil one. We know also that the Son of God has come and has given us understanding, so that we may know him who is true. And we are in him who is true by being in his Son Jesus Christ. He is the true God and eternal life.
>
> (1 John 5:19–20)

Let's move on now to our outward focus.

Messengers of warning and of hope

Here the Holy Spirit is at work as the world's prosecutor, but the point is that he works in and through the disciples' testimony before the world. Yet he speaks through them also of the world's Saviour, proclaiming peace and reconciliation, offering forgiveness because now is the day of salvation (Luke 4:16–21).

Here's a thought to take with us through the weeks and years ahead: that where we go, the Spirit goes, and where we speak for Jesus Christ, the Spirit speaks. Too often we are timid and apologetic in our Christian witness, but remember that whenever we declare who Jesus Christ is, and what he has done, it is a significant event. Unbelievers may be uninterested and even indignant, but they have been charged by the Spirit of truth with the facts that are being proclaimed. Remember, it is not you who is on trial, but they.

Our great Helper in all of this is the Holy Spirit, who goes out from the Father and is sent by the Son to testify in every generation and society that Jesus Christ is the Son of God and Saviour, and to draw men and women and children to him. Christlikeness is not only a personal development; it is a public commitment. As such, it involves following the Holy Spirit where he leads, and his leading can be in the unfamiliar situations that confront us, or the familiar people who surround us.

Ours is a university city, and our church has many students. They live in a campus world of challenge, but also in families where the same call to Christlike cooperation with the Holy Spirit comes to them – often at the start of their Christian lives. A couple of years ago Christians in the universities were engaged in a mission called *Uncover*. Tens of thousands of copies of Luke's Gospel were printed, interleaved with pages for notes, and Christians were urged to offer to go through Luke with friends who were not believers.

One student who gave his life to the Lord immediately called his parents with the news that he had become a Christian. Not quite knowing how to respond, they said, 'That's interesting. Now what would you like for Christmas?' He answered, 'I just want one thing. Would you and Dad go through the *Uncover* study with me when I'm home? That's all I want for Christmas.' Wonderful! No embarrassment, no avoidance, no sheltering in anonymity; he had found the greatest good news in the world, and he wanted to share it with others.

In our land many voices are raised, and every kind of view is expressed and defended. In the public square the Christian voice must not fall silent, for our message is the most urgent and important of all. But behind that, giving authenticity to it, there must be lives in which the Holy Spirit is creating the beauty of Jesus Christ who is the image of God. For this we were made, by the one who said in the beginning, 'Let us make mankind in our image, in our likeness' (Genesis 1:26). In Christ he is making men and women in a fallen world part of his new creation (2 Corinthians 5:17; Ephesians 4:24; Colossians 3:10).

Recovering 'true vertical'

In his fine commentary on John, Gary Burge recalls C. S. Lewis's novel *That Hideous Strength* and the point in it when angelic beings from 'deep heaven' called 'Eldils' begin their descent and siege of earth:

> Suddenly they appear in dazzling brightness in Ransom's quarters. They are like shining pillars of light, powerful and dangerous, spinning at a speed he cannot fathom. But the important part lies here: They are not exactly vertical columns but seem to stand about ten degrees off. The impression Ransom has, however, is not that they are 'off 10 degrees' but that they are in fact connected to 'true vertical' and that the entire world is 'off 10 degrees'. For the first time Ransom sees 'true vertical', and it makes the entire world seem irregular. Forever Ransom knows that the floor is not quite level . . .

One mission of the church, therefore, is to be the *one* voice that holds an honest assessment of the world, that speaks of the way it twists the meaning of sin, righteousness and judgment, and that describes boldly its absence of justice and compassion, and its failure to promote true virtue in the fear of God. The church's testimony should uncover 'true vertical' so that the world can see how it has skewed our reality. This is the courageous testimony that the Spirit seeks to engage and empower.[2]

Our children have to learn this too.

'Dad, is Uncle John a Christian?'

I remember one of my children asking me this many years ago as he lay in bed one night. Now, John was a neighbour, the father of another child who shared the school run with us. I knew that I must answer carefully: if I said he was, then I would not be telling the truth; he was not a believer. But if I simply said he was not a Christian, I would not be doing justice to aspects of his character and life. I knew that early on I had to start to prepare my son for the realities of future life in this area.

So I said carefully, 'Well, uncle so-and so is a good husband and father, as you know, and a very nice man. He's nice to most people, and he's very nice to us, isn't he?' My son nodded vigorously. 'But you know,' I continued, 'he's not nice to God.' He looked incredulous; he probably thought all nice people were Christians, and of course that included all family friends.

'No,' I said, 'Uncle John doesn't want God in his life, and he doesn't want to know about Jesus. And you will find that a lot of people are like that. That's why we need to pray for people that God will change their hearts, and for their children that they will grow up to know about Jesus.'

It was an early lesson in the hostility that Jesus Christ still meets in the world.

Later on in their lives this will become more important to our children as they prepare to meet the scorn that being a Christian often attracts, or the resentment, the throwaway comment that comes like a slap in the face. We must let them know that these people too need Jesus, and they need to stand firm for their faith and pray for them. Perhaps one day the children who laugh will respect them, and even come to them for help. They really must be prepared to be in the minority and to stand firm against peer pressures.

Years later when we were leaving that part of the city and I had prayed that we might know that our witness to the neighbours had not been in vain, the daughter of 'Uncle John', now an adult and away from home, wrote to ask us about Christianity and how she could know God in her life 'because', she said 'you were always so nice to us'.

We simply do not know what God will do with our witness as followers of the Lord Jesus. As believers, we are called to shine like stars in the world (Philippians 2:15). But stars suggest darkness, and we see their light in the night, not the day. So our light must shine, and our testimony to God and his Christ must persist in a world of contradictions. Yes, and even in the knowledge of our own inadequacy and unworthiness!

12

Facing the contradictions within ourselves

A major feature of the Christian life is the struggle with sin and temptation. In his book *Temptation*, Charles Durham writes:

> I am convinced that there is more temptation in our day than ever before. It is increasing in several ways. First, it is increasing in sheer amount . . . Second, to yield to temptation is increasingly accepted . . . Third, temptation has increased in intensity. The appeals to greed are brighter and slicker . . . Fourth, temptation has increased in pervasiveness . . . Fifth, temptation has increased in persuasiveness. We are told that there are good reasons, based on science, psychology and sociology, for forgetting the old rules of behaviour.[1]

We like to think of ourselves as being in control of what we do, but when we do wrong, evil very soon gets out of control. The rumour we started travels on, and we cannot recall it; the lie we said demands another lie to protect it; the unkindness we showed is remembered and perhaps passed on to others; the ruthless business decision, stupid flirtation, the convenient affair, all have knock-on effects and even a life of their own.

Sin is not the end of a matter; it has consequences, breeding further and stronger sins. In the end it leads to death – hopeless, endless, Godless death – an eternal desolation. I have never forgotten these words by Steve Farrar, in his fine book *Finishing Strong*:

> Sin will take you farther than you wanted to go.
> Sin will keep you longer than you wanted to stay.
> Sin will cost you more than you wanted to pay.[2]

The old writers used to speak of the world, the flesh and the devil as the three great enemies of the Christian and Christian living. Tradition has 'the seven deadly sins' as pride, envy, anger, sloth, avarice, gluttony and lust. We may be more strongly tempted along some of these lines than others, and tempted more strongly at some times and in some situations than others. At such times we urgently need to renew our first surrender to Christ as Lord. We used to sing a song which included the line: 'Lift your hands in sweet surrender to his name', and in the church service it was easy, but the time to do it again and with fresh urgency is at those times when temptations come in like a flood.

There was only ever one perfect example of resisting temptation.

Jesus in temptation

Jesus was no stranger to temptation. If C. S. Lewis is right, then our Lord knew the force of temptation more than we ever shall do. He writes:

Only those who try to resist temptation know how strong
it is . . . A man who gives in to temptation after five minutes
simply does not know what it would have been like an hour
later. That is why bad people, in one sense, know very little
about badness. They have lived a sheltered life by always giving
in. We never find out the strength of the evil impulse inside us
until we try to fight it: and Christ, because He was the only
man who never yielded to temptation, is also the only man
who knows to the full what temptation means – the only
complete realist.[3]

His greatest temptation was along the line of his calling –
especially to choose a way other than that of the cross. Jesus
was tempted in this way at the beginning of his public
ministry (Matthew 4:1), and he was tempted at its end too
(Mark 14:34). He saw Peter move from being a mouthpiece
of God to being a mouthpiece of Satan (Matthew 16:16–17,
21–23), and he saw all the disciples flee in terror where they
should have stood in solidarity with him (Mark 14:50). His
warning to his followers was to, 'Watch and pray so that
you will not enter into temptation' (Mark 14:38). Only he
knew the horror of all he had before him, yet he went on:
'Abba, Father . . . everything is possible for you. Take this
cup from me. Yet not what I will, but what you will' (Mark
14:36).

Out of the wide range of temptations that beset and often
entrap the Christian believer I have chosen just one here, but
it is one we all know too well. For Christians in our Western
societies today one of the most potent and persistent forms
of temptation is along the lines of our sexuality, so I will
focus on this as an example, although I'm well aware that
there are many others that hinder our witness and ensnare
our lives.

Christlikeness in sexual faithfulness

We all know that some of the deepest and most powerful contradictions of Christlikeness in our lives relate to our sexuality and the enormous assaults from our over-sexualized society. What is Jesus' and the wider biblical teaching about this?

As we might expect, the Bible does not have a low view of sex, but a high one. What it speaks against, repeatedly and consistently, is the disorder of our sexuality since the fall and on account of sin. Something uniquely good and God-blessed has been exaggerated, misdirected and badly managed.

Good sex is about love, not just sexual drive, about commitment to another, not just self-satisfying desire, and about children too, who are often unmentioned in fashionable articles on sexual liberation. Bad sex is about lust and loneliness and exploitation. Lust is not desire, but desire wrongly directed, is not about sexual drive, but about sexual abuse: about using people for sexual relief or sexual entertainment or mere power games. It's about watching pornography, which depersonalizes people, treating them as mere sex objects; it's about degrading individuals in your mind with thoughts that include them in sexual activity to which they would never consent in real life.

It's never 'just sex'

Jesus understood this and warned that there were forces in the human heart that were corrupt and destructive, rendering one offensive ('unclean') before God: 'For it is from within, out of a person's heart, that evil thoughts come – sexual immorality, theft, murder, adultery, greed, malice, deceit, lewdness, envy, slander, arrogance and folly' (Mark 7:21–22).

Notice how sexual sin is repeatedly prominent in the list. These things are not merely human failings, but human corruptions. They cause serious offence to God and produce serious consequences among people.

Notice too the connections that exist between sexual sin and other forms of sin in this list. Sexual sins are often aroused by other sins, such as envy and greed, and they can lead to other sins such as deceit, violence and even murder. Sin does not exist alone; it is 'remarkably generative',[4] and one set of sins easily leads to another.

That is why a society that becomes conveniently permissive in one area will become uncomfortably, even menacingly, permissive in another. Sexual misbehaviour gives rise to jealousies and disappointments, resentments and even violence. Guy Brandon has written a very fine book on this subject, entitled *Just Sex?*, with the subtitle *Is it ever just sex?*[5]

Soon after the permissive sixties one social commentator warned that if sex were regarded as casual, it would lead to a situation where many would regard rape as no great matter. Today we often read about charges of date rape in court where it is clear that many do not know how to read the 'signals' any more. Signals are no substitute for rules, and when rules are thrown out, then confusion comes in. As G. K. Chesterton once pointed out to his readers, before you remove a fence, it's wise to find out why it was put there in the first place.

Sex is relational

The detachment of sex from deep relations with mutual obligations is extremely damaging to our society. Sex is relational – it was always meant to be – affecting persons, not just bodies, and affecting society, not only individuals. It's been said that the question used to be: 'How many times do you go out with a person before you have sex with them?' Now the question is quite likely to be: 'How many times do you have to have sex with a person before you can say you are in a relationship with them?'

Sophisticated people have sometimes spoken of their 'open' marriages. But they were only open as a wound is open to infection. In our society today there are huge numbers of adults and children who suffer from the fallout of marital unfaithfulness and divorce, carrying the scars for a lifetime. We hear a great deal about safe sex today, but this reminds us that, in the words of writer Norman Mailer, 'There is nothing safe about sex. There never will be.'

Jesus' concern was that we guard our inner lives and thoughts as the way to keep ourselves free of such entanglement: 'You have heard that it was said, "You shall not commit adultery." But I tell you that anyone who looks at a woman lustfully has already committed adultery with her in his heart' (Matthew 5:27–28). The seventh commandment, 'Do not commit adultery', was given not to prohibit sex, but to protect marriage, and Jesus' words do not focus on sexual attraction as such, but 'on the desire for (and perhaps the planning of) an illicit sexual liaison'.[6] This is in the spirit of the tenth commandment and in particular the warning, 'You shall not covet your neighbour's wife' (Exodus 20:17).

Cobwebs becoming cables

People in wrong relationships sometimes say, 'We tried to fight it, but the attraction was too strong for us.' But there was a time when it was not strong at all and the other person was only noticed with a flicker of approval or pleasure. The issue could easily have been dealt with then: you can't help the first look, but you can help the second and the third, and the thoughts that are entertained, perhaps played with, becoming fantasies and becoming a plan and a seduction. Cobwebs become cables in such cases, and what could have been brushed aside with ease or broken through in the early stages now becomes a trap and a prison.

If you find yourself increasingly attracted to an unsuitable person, then you should avoid them in whatever ways you can. They may be in the next office, and you can't help seeing them, but if they have coffee at a certain time and place, you can have it at another time and in another place, or can at least occupy the time with someone else. You cannot pray, 'Lead us not into temptation' if you lead yourself into temptation. 'If step one to marital unfaithfulness is "just thoughts", then step two can be emotional non-physical involvement, where physical adultery is not even contemplated but where complete emotional involvement can be just as damaging. A line is crossed between honest friendship and inappropriate involvement.'[7]

There may be some friendships that must fade or even cease, some relationships that must cool because they are becoming too warm, because emotional non-physical involvement can threaten a marriage as effectively as adultery if the wife or husband is not appropriately involved. In short, marriages must be uniquely guarded and protected by husband and wife working together.

There may be a friendship that troubles your spouse, and perhaps your friends, and while you yourself may feel safe in it, you should draw back to safer limits. You do not know the contradictions of your own heart, and you do not know the contradictions of that other person's heart either. No one has the right to risk another person's feelings and be implicated in their downfall.

The stare of the snake

In *The Life God Blesses* Gordon MacDonald writes a chapter on the power of sin called 'The Stare of the Snake' and relates the experience of Carlos Villas, a Spanish monk who has lived much of his life in India.

> Villas tells of a bicycle ride and a strange experience in the Indian countryside. He had become aware of an unusual silence in which all the normal noises and motions of nature seemed to come to a halt. At first there was no discernible explanation, and he was puzzled.
>
> But then, Villas says, he saw something off to one side, and the mystery became clear. There, not far from where the monk stood with his bicycle, was a snake, its head slowly bobbing and weaving as it fixed upon a small bird perched on a lower branch of a shrub. The bird seemed paralysed, as if locked in a hypnotic trance by the snake's motions. It appeared incapable of flight.
>
> Villas braced in anticipation of the snake's strike, wondering at the same time if there was something he could do to save the ill-fated bird. Then, knowing no other alternative, he attempted to distract the snake by rushing towards it, waving his arms and shouting loudly . . . The effort was successful. The snake's arresting stare was broken, and the bird – free of the 'hypnosis' – instantly spread its wings and leaped skyward.[8]

Sometimes we are held by a temptation, transfixed by a fear, unable to tear ourselves away from a dangerous situation. And it requires God to send someone bursting in on you with flailing arms and a loud voice crying, 'Stop! Do not conform any longer to the pattern of this world.' It may be the Holy

Spirit using the warnings of the preacher at church, the worried tones of a friend, or a text with some words from the Bible. It may even be right now, from this section of this book! God has ways of breaking the stare of the snake.

That, however, is an emergency. God is concerned to keep us from getting into such extreme situations in the first place.

The tug-of-war

> So I say, live by the Spirit, and you will not gratify the desires
> of the flesh. For the flesh desires what is contrary to the
> Spirit, and the Spirit what is contrary to the flesh. They are
> in conflict with each other, so that you are not to do whatever
> you want. But if you are led by the Spirit, you are not under
> the law.
> (Galatians 5:16–18)

Dr Jim Packer has some very good things to say about these verses in *Keep in Step with the Spirit*. These words, he writes,

> alert us to the reality of tension, the necessity of effort,
> and the incompleteness of achievement that mark the life
> of holiness in the world . . . The anti-God energy that
> indwelling sin repeatedly looses in the form of temptations,
> delusions and distractions keeps total perfection beyond
> our grasp.[9]

He writes earlier:

> Paul is telling us here in Galatians about the reality of conflict
> in the Christian life. You must realize, he says, that there are
> two opposed sorts of desire in every Christian's make-up.

The opposition between them appears at the level of motive. There are desires that express the natural anti-God egoism of fallen human nature and there are desires that express the supernatural, God-honouring, God-loving motivation that is implanted by new birth.[10]

He later speaks of the experience (a distressing one to the Christian) of finding in oneself 'allergically negative reactions and responses' to God's will, which means that sin, though 'dethroned is not destroyed, though doomed to die is not yet dead'.[11] We see these things within us, and we can begin to doubt that we are really a Christian at all. But Paul makes it clear that we also have in us, in that same self, the Holy Spirit of God fighting the temptation, and helping us to fight it we have what he calls 'the spirit of adoption' (see Romans 8:15, ESV) – the spirit of sons and daughters.

To our deep relief, we find that the pull of sin, the pressure of temptation, does not signify our hopelessness or our unconverted state, or our 'true selves', because it meets in us this contrary force: the pull towards goodness, righteousness and purity, the strong desire to walk with God, a real hatred of the very sin that works within our nature. The conflict is not a sign of hypocrisy or falseness, but a sign that we are the true children of God, struggling to leave behind the old life and submit to God for discipline and training, as well as for healing a damaged and sinful humanity which is saved and in the process of being sanctified.

The Spirit gives power to oppose and overcome sin, and live godly and righteous lives in faith and love. The believer is not 'the helpless battle-ground of two opposing forces'.[12] We know whose side we are on, as well as who is at our side in the struggle. We are children of light who hate the patches of darkness within our hearts and minds. And we are being led by the kindest, wisest, most patient and long-suffering Friend anyone could have: the Holy Spirit himself.

One day we will be free for ever from the 'contradictions' that frustrate us in this life. It is to that wonderful reality that we finally turn.

Part 5
The triumph of Christlikeness

13

The return with Christ

He is coming again!

The truth of the Second Coming of Christ to save his church and judge the world is prominent throughout the New Testament: it is believed by every writer, stated in almost every book and applied to almost every aspect of the Christian life. We might say that if the New Testament *landscape* is dominated by the cross, then the New Testament *horizon* is dominated by the return of the Lord.

In his first coming he came in lowliness and obscurity – the baby of Bethlehem, the Man of Calvary. At his second coming he will come in cosmic power and divine glory – the Lord of heaven. In his first coming he came as the Saviour of his people; at his second coming he will come as Judge of all the world.

In many of his parables and sayings Jesus used various dramatic pictures to illustrate and express his return in its different aspects. He said it would be sudden and universal judgment, like the flood that swept a world away. He warned that it would be unexpected and startling, like the entry of a thief in the night taking many unprepared. He said that it would be a personal call to accountability, examination and evaluation to everyone who had ever lived, like the return of a master calling his servants to account (Matthew 24:36–51; 25:14–30).

But he also said that, for a watching, waiting, faithful church, it would be like the coming of a bridegroom for his bride, with all the glory and joy and music of heaven (Matthew 25:1–13).

Christlikeness watches and works

Jesus ended one parable about his return with these words: 'Therefore keep watch, because you do not know on what day your Lord will come' (Matthew 24:42).

'Keep watch' is literally 'keep awake', and involves not simply a mental attitude, but a moral quality of spiritual readiness for the Lord's return: 'You also must be ready' (verse 44). It is not a case of calculating how near the return of Christ may be, but of living in readiness for it. Of course such readiness is not a matter of living in a state of constant anxiety, or on 'red alert', but of living the kind of life that pleases the Lord, and so, in that way, being prepared for his coming at any time, waking or sleeping, working or worshipping.

'Keeping watch' here is not like waiting at a bus stop, but working at your job, living with your family, witnessing in the world, faithfully looking to the coming Lord and Judge for your vindication and for his 'Well done, good and faithful servant'.

The Bible brings almost every aspect of life to focus on this final truth of human history. Try looking up the following Bible texts and passages, all a great encouragement to day-by-day godliness: 1 Thessalonians 1:10; 2:13; 3:13; 5:23;

Titus 2:11–14. It is a focus in all church life and worship (1 Corinthians 1:7; 11:26; Hebrews 10:25). It is the Christian's confidence in spiritual warfare (Romans 13:11–13; 16:20; 1 Corinthians 6:3; 1 Thessalonians 5:2–8; 2 Thessalonians 2:8–12). It is the believer's comfort in times of persecution (Romans 8:18–25; 2 Thessalonians 1:6–10). And it is the survivor's great consolation at the loss of loved ones (1 Thessalonians 4:13–18).

Hope in the appearing of Christ is accordingly 'the distinguishing mark of the Christian life'.[1]

The people of God must be fully prepared for that great event. We must not lose the working in the watching, nor must we lose the watching in the working.

Certain, sudden and soon

When I was a boy, preachers on the subject often had three favourite points when they spoke of the Second Coming. They said it will be *certain*, *sudden* and *soon*. And so it will be, according to Scripture. But then frequently they went off on a line of their own, adding up signs and dates and international events and odd interpretations of various texts, and sometimes they held fierce debates about what would happen before and after this or that.

However, next to the certainty of the event, in the New Testament teaching, its *imminence*, its 'soon-ness', is very important in the shaping of the church's life and Christians' lives in every generation.

Though God's patience has held it off for more than 2,000 years, it is always true that each generation stands in the place of the last. And each generation of believers must live as though it was indeed the last, ready for the coming of their Lord and Saviour Jesus Christ.

A planned and timed delay

Among the first generation of believers no one could have known that God's plan was at least 2,000 years long. They simply expected 'the last days' to be short, and the end of all things to coincide with their own lifetimes. Consequently, as the years went by since the death and resurrection of Jesus, questions of different kinds arose in and around the young churches. For instance, there were the 'scoffers' that Peter writes of in his second letter who said, 'Where is this "coming" he promised?' (2 Peter 3:3–4).

However, it is clear that the delay is a crucially important part of the divine plan, since it provides the time in which millions will be gathered into the kingdom of God from every tribe and language and people and nation (Revelation 5:9). As Peter says, 'The Lord is not slow in keeping his promise, as some understand slowness. Instead he is patient with you, not wanting anyone to perish, but everyone to come to repentance' (2 Peter 3:9).

A certain glory

Among the Thessalonian Christians there was a degree of consternation as, one after another, believers died who would not be alive on earth when the Lord returned. Would they miss out in some way? Paul writes in his first letter to them:

> For we believe that Jesus died and rose again, and so we believe that God will bring with Jesus those who have fallen asleep in him. According to the Lord's word, we tell you that we who are still alive, who are left until the coming of the Lord, will certainly not precede those who have fallen asleep.

For the Lord himself will come down from heaven, with a loud command, with the voice of the archangel and with the trumpet call of God, and the dead in Christ will rise first.
(1 Thessalonians 4:14–16)

Notice how he moves from the death and resurrection of our Lord to his return, and our part in it, in those first words: 'We believe that Jesus died and rose again, and so we believe that God will bring with Jesus those who have fallen asleep in him.' It is the first coming of Christ Jesus that guarantees the second. What he *has done* is the basis of what he *will do*. His victory at the cross and his subsequent resurrection from the dead are the guarantee of the final triumph over sin and death and the restitution of all things. His own resurrection is the guarantee of ours.

And what of the living at the coming of Christ? 'After that, we who are still alive and are left will be caught up together with them in the clouds to meet the Lord in the air. And so we will be with the Lord for ever' (1 Thessalonians 4:17). Clouds are often the sign of the divine presence in the Old Testament. The clouds here are not the clouds of the meteorologist, but the visible glory of God. What we have is the immediate transformation of the old body into the new, and the entrance into the glory of God of those who are still on earth when the Lord comes.

Our bodies, Paul says, will not be struck lifeless, but caught up into the eternal glory of the coming Lord, no longer mundane but heavenly, no longer sick or old or limited, but spiritual and glorious and immortal after the pattern of Christ's own resurrection body (1 Corinthians 15:49–54), no longer limited to earth, but unlimited in future possibilities.

It is strange that believers can 'encourage one another' (1 Thessalonians 4:18) in view of an event so cosmic, so disruptive of every human institution, so different from anything we have known before. How will we cope?

Little boy lost

As a small child I went with my mother on holiday to the home of an aunt who lived near Manchester. One day we were taken into the city and into Lewis's department store (no relation of mine unfortunately!). I had never seen a department store like it before and I was staggered at the size. Not only was it bigger than any of the shops I'd known in my village (all twelve of them); it was bigger than all of them put together.

The first call was for a haircut for me. I was placed on a giraffe, I think, or it might have been a zebra, to have my hair cut. (Our village barber used his front room!) I was then taken in tow while my mother and her sister moved steadily from department to department. The crowds were daunting, but I held on tightly to my mother's coat and felt quite safe.

Then at one point, I wanted to say something to her and looked up – only to find myself looking into the face of an old woman I had never seen before in my life. I had been holding on to the wrong coat! I still remember the utter panic of realizing that I was lost in a strange city, hundreds of miles from my home, and in a store that seemed bigger than my entire village. I would never find my mother and aunt, and in years to come they would find my bleached bones lying somewhere in the haberdashery department.

In panic I spun round in the crowd – only to find my mother and aunt standing behind me, both of them smiling broadly! They had been following me and the old woman, wondering when I would realize what I had done. The wave of panic was instantly banished by the wave of relief that washed over me at the smiling face of my mother. All the world was in that face, and I was safe.

I have sometimes thought it will be like that for those of us who are still on earth when the Lord comes at the end of history. In the wreck of worlds and the panic of millions we read in the book of Revelation:

> Then the kings of the earth, the princes, the generals, the rich, the mighty, and everyone else . . . called to the mountains and the rocks, 'Fall on us and hide us from the face of him who sits on the throne and from the wrath of the Lamb!' (Revelation 6:15–16)

Perhaps momentarily we too will be filled with fear, but when we look up to the face 'of him who sits on the throne', *we shall know it*: we shall know it as the face of our own dear Saviour, and we will respond to his love with our own.

As we study the New Testament teaching, we learn that there are two great events that immediately follow the Second Coming: the resurrection of the dead, and the final judgment.

Christlike in our resurrection bodies

We do not often think of the resurrection of the body, but in the New Testament the salvation of believers is never simply a matter of the salvation of their souls. In Romans 8:23 Paul writes, 'we wait eagerly for . . . the redemption of our bodies.' In Jesus Christ his Son, God achieved a complete victory over the ruin sin had made in his universe. He signalled that the victory of Christ would be repeated in us. Christ was raised in body, and so shall we be.

In one of his best-loved sayings Jesus promised, 'I am the resurrection and the life. The one who believes in me will live, even though they die; and whoever lives by believing in me will never die' (John 11:25–26). Jesus did not only say, 'I am the life' but also 'I am *the resurrection* and the life.' He was referring to the general resurrection, a doctrine widely believed in by Jews of the time (John 11:24), but Jesus pointed to himself and his own resurrection as its meaning and power.

To the Philippians Paul writes:

> our citizenship is in heaven. And we eagerly await a Saviour from there, the Lord Jesus Christ, who, by the power that enables him to bring everything under his control, will transform our lowly bodies so that they will be like his glorious body.
> (Philippians 3:20)

The glorified body of the risen Jesus is the model of what ours will be.

Like him at last!

A short while ago one of my sons was speaking to me of a Christian man whom I had met only a few times, but whom he knew well as he had been at school with his son. We had both known him as a strong, burly, confident, cultured man, active for many years in his church, and with a deep interest in classical music and the opera. But now, years later, age and severe illness had taken their toll, and he was skin and bones, unable to walk without help. 'Dad,' said my son, 'you wouldn't know him; he's just a shadow of his former self.'

We all know that phrase and that sad reality – common in our world as it is. But here is the astounding announcement, the great reversal. As Tom Wright has put it, we hear people saying, 'He's just a shadow of his former self', but the great truth about followers of Christ is that 'who we are at the moment is just a shadow of our future selves'.[2] However strong we are or have been, however beautiful, however learned, however wise, however good, it is nothing compared to how we shall be. We are only a shadow of our future selves!

This new body, says Paul in 1 Corinthians 15, will be imperishable, glorious and powerful. What came to the grave in weakness, disfigurement and indignity will be raised in power and beauty and honour:

> So will it be with the resurrection of the dead. The body that is sown is perishable, it is raised imperishable; it is sown in dishonour, it is raised in glory; it is sown in weakness, it is raised in power; it is sown a natural body, it is raised a spiritual body . . . And just as we have borne the image of the earthly man, so shall we bear the image of the heavenly man.
> (1 Corinthians 15:42–44, 49)

And the glory that shall rest on us will be his glory, the beauty that we shall see in each other will be his beauty, the likeness of Christ in every face.

As the apostle John writes in his first letter, 'Dear friends, now we are children of God, and what we will be has not yet been made known. But we know that when Christ appears, *we shall be like him*, for we shall see him as he is' (1 John 3:2, italics mine).

Christlikeness and the Last Judgment

After the resurrection the Last Judgment will take place.

The Last Judgment will be a time in which all will be judged: every life evaluated of both the saved and the lost. In the Old Testament God is the Judge of all the earth, it is the prerogative of Deity, but in the New Testament we learn from

Jesus himself that all judgment has been entrusted to the Son: 'the Father judges no one, but has entrusted all judgment to the Son, that all may honour the Son just as they honour the Father' (John 5:22–23).

Those who belong to Christ will be judged, but we will be judged as God's already-saved people, saved by the full atonement of Christ, our sins forgiven, our eternal destiny certain. But we will still be judged in terms of how we have used the grace and the gifts of God.

Rewards and losses

As Jesus said in various sayings and parables, it will be a time of rewards and losses, of examination and congratulation, of approval and reproof, of greater and lesser glory (Matthew 25:14–23). Some Christians will be saved, but with great loss, for instance, certain church leaders in 1 Corinthians 3 who built their own little kingdoms, divided fellowships and even ruined churches to satisfy their own ambitions and egos (see 3:15).

Others will receive in full the rewards Jesus promised: 'Blessed are you when people insult you, persecute you and falsely say all kinds of evil against you because of me. Rejoice and be glad, because great is your reward in heaven' (Matthew 5:11–12). The apostle Paul continues the teaching of Jesus on this matter: 'For we must all appear before the judgment seat of Christ, so that each of us may receive what is due to us for the things done while in the body, whether good or bad' (2 Corinthians 5:10).

A gentle judgment?

All of us will be examined and our lives evaluated. Yet both Paul and John say we can have confidence on the day of judgment (2 Corinthians 5:5, 8; 1 John 4:17). Why? Because, says Paul, 'the one who has fashioned us for this very purpose is God'. Because, says John, the love our heavenly Father has for us and all his people is immeasurable, and because that love has come to lie in the depths of our hearts so that 'in this world we are like Jesus', and because in that day what he has begun in us will be perfected.

The judgment of each believer will be impartial, but not impersonal; it will be honest, but not brutal; it will be the judgment of our Saviour and our Friend. He will take into account every extenuating factor and every stressful circumstance, every struggle and every pressure, and most of all he will fulfil the love he has always had for us.

In this connection I sometimes think of a father and his young son at the end of the day sitting together on a sofa, with the father's arm around the son. He is taking the child through the day, its ups and downs, including mistakes and some bad behaviour. He is encouraging, and even congratulating, his child at certain points, while at others he is correcting him and showing his disapproval. 'Now why did you do that?' or 'Why did you say that?' or 'Wouldn't it have been better if you had done it like this?'

He will ask us why we did not do certain things and why we did do others – and we shall not be able to take refuge in false excuses. We shall be ashamed at our failures and sins, but we shall be amazed at his mercy and forgiveness. For the result of the judgment of the saved will be the level of honour and glory they enter, and this will be more for some than others, although I believe we will all advance through eternity. So we can look with confidence, as well as humility, to what is before us (2 Corinthians 5:1–10; 1 John 3:1–3).

However, there will be some for whom judgment will not be gentle, including those who have abused their trust as leaders of the churches, and who will be saved 'only as one escaping through the flames' (1 Corinthians 3:15).

The end of evil

The final judgment will also include those who have resisted God and the gospel, rebelling without surrender against their Maker and his lordship. It will be the convicting assessment of lives where God has been left out, or where other gods have taken his place. It will be the day when great wickedness will meet with terrible wrath, but also where the secrets of all hearts will be laid bare so that no one will be able to accuse God of injustice (Romans 2:16; Revelation 20:11–12).

All this is important because it is the truth of the final judgment that gives moral weight and ultimate meaning to our everyday lives; it tells us that everything counts, that no good thing is missed, no act of love and service forgotten – and no unatoned-for wickedness is hidden from God (Matthew 25:31–46). The doctrine of the Last Judgment should be affirmed without embarrassment by the church in every generation, making it clear that the moral choices we make day by day have eternal significance.

As C. S. Lewis memorably put it, 'In the end that Face which is the delight or the terror of the universe must be turned upon each of us . . . either conferring glory inexpressible or inflicting shame that can never be cured or disguised.'[3]

14

Christlike at last!

After the general judgment the people of God will be led into a new and never-ending story in a new heavens and a new earth.

Christlike in a new heaven and on a new earth

This is how the Bible ends:

> Then I saw 'a new heaven and a new earth,' for the first heaven and the first earth had passed away, and there was no longer any sea. I saw the Holy City, the new Jerusalem, coming down out of heaven from God, prepared as a bride beautifully dressed for her husband. And I heard a loud voice from the throne saying, 'Look! God's dwelling-place is now among the people, and he will dwell with them. They will be his people, and God himself will be with them and be their God. "He will wipe every tear from their eyes. There will be no more death" or mourning or crying or pain, for the old order of things has passed away.'

> He who was seated on the throne said, 'I am making
> everything new!' Then he said, 'Write this down, for these
> words are trustworthy and true.'
>   He said to me: 'It is done. I am the Alpha and the Omega,
> the Beginning and the End.'
> (Revelation 21:1–6)

The 'Holy City' of Revelation 21:2 is not bricks and stone, but
people – us! Not us as we are, but as we shall be, humanity as
it was always intended to be: men and women in the image
of God, in the likeness of Christ, and children who have
never grown up in any other world but this new one, where
touching symbols become greater realities (e.g. Zechariah 8:5;
Matthew 18:10).

What a marvellous ending, what a triumph of grace
and salvation, what a destiny that each of us can look forward to!

The last word of God's Word is joy – the joy of an eternal
salvation, the joy of a full redemption, the joy of becoming
all we were meant to be. It gathers up all the broken notes of
the first creation, when 'the morning stars sang together and
all the angels shouted for joy' (Job 38:7), and raises the first
and spoiled creation into a redemption that reaches to the
farthest parts of the cosmos. 'Then I saw "a new heaven and
a new earth"' (Revelation 21:1).

Our material faith!

Someone has said that the Christian faith is the most material-
istic of all the religions. By that, they meant that the biblical
doctrine of creation and the biblical hope of the new creation
affirm the goodness of the created order and the materiality
of life.

This was in strong contrast with much of the thinking of Greek philosophy and many of the religions of the ancient (and modern) world. There the spiritual is elevated, and the physical is denigrated. Some forms of Greek thinking saw the physical body as a necessary encumbrance to be sloughed off at death, releasing the imprisoned spirit. Some Eastern religions and philosophies saw matter as essentially evil, and death as a release from it. Only the spirit mattered.

But biblical revelation stands in stark contrast to all that from the beginning, and eventually it helped to pioneer a new attitude to the sick and the disabled.

Bodies matter too

With the Christian outlook, and its growth and spread in the Roman Empire, the beginning of the large-scale organized care of the sick had come. It came most strongly in the fourth century, after Christians had suffered much discrimination, poverty and persecution, and when they were able to organize and practise openly. That century would see the first large hospitals filled with plague victims, leprosy sufferers, the poor and the aged, built by outstanding Christian leaders like Basil of Caesarea and Ephraim of Edessa.

Why? Why did Fabiola, a fifth-century Mother Teresa, and others, gather the sick from the streets and nurse sufferers wasted with poverty and disease? Because faith believed God's evaluation of them, and love went out to claim them for a future that hope saw clearly when others did not. Because Christianity embraced those who were excluded, with its message of the cross and its conviction that God had chosen the weak things of the world to shame the strong (1 Corinthians 1:26–27).

Some years ago an obituary appeared in *The Times* on the life of Grace Bennett, an outstanding missionary nurse who carried out pioneering work among leprosy sufferers in South Korea from the mid-1950s with the Leprosy Mission. Grace Bennett's team had more than a thousand patients, and they saw up to 700 each month as they made the rounds of the clinics and travelled many miles.

The patients were always waiting, and after giving them the traditional Korean greeting: 'Are you in peace?', they would then take part in a short Christian service before the clinic got to work. Grace died aged eighty-six, having been awarded the OBE in 1975. She said at the time,

> One of the special rewards of this work is that we see people who come to the hospital as physical and spiritual wrecks, full of hopelessness . . . and then we find they can be cured. We watch them begin to regain their dignity as human beings, and also have the privilege of helping them come to know Jesus Christ.[1]

Our well-earthed hope

Genesis tells us that God saw all he had made, and it was good. The psalmist could say he was 'fearfully and wonderfully made' (Psalm 139:14). Prophets like Isaiah looked forward to the renewal of the earth. Towards the end of Isaiah's prophecy God says, 'See, I will create new heavens and new earth. The former things will not be remembered, nor will they come to mind' (Isaiah 65:17).

By New Testament times 'the new earth became a familiar topic of Jewish end-time discussion',[2] and John takes up that theme in part using Isaiah's marvellous imagery.

Unfortunately, just as Greek thinking impacted on the later church, so the ancient Greek divorce between matter and spirit captured the thinking of many Christians, and has done right up to the present. Hardly anyone speaks of the new earth these days. Instead, they speak of 'heaven', which is a far vaguer concept, and the idea has become almost universal that we will all be spirits in heaven for the rest of eternity.

But the biblical teaching, so clearly set forth here, is that our disembodied state in heaven after we die is only preparatory until the Second Coming (2 Corinthians 5:1–10). What will follow will be the resurrection of the dead, that is, the giving of resurrection bodies to Christ's people, and their life on a real planet as part of a real creation, reflecting the wisdom and power of their Creator who 'saw all that he had made, and it was very good' (Genesis 1:31). I do not know what other worlds this may involve, but I do know that they will be God's worlds in God's new creation.

'Tell me there'll be kites to fly'

And as for this world, if it is beautiful now, what will it be like then? In Romans 8 Paul speaks of all creation waiting in eager expectation for when nature itself will be liberated from its bondage to decay (see verses 21–23). And we ourselves were made for this kind of world: mountains and valleys, seas and cities, laughter and activity, worship and work. No wonder we are reluctant to leave this world, even for heaven: we were made for such a world as this, not programmed for death. There is a dash of good theology in Adrian Plass's moving poem 'Christmas in Heaven', in which he expresses his longing to know some of the joys of his earthly existence when he reaches heaven (flying kites being one) – after all, he confesses, this world is all he knows.

Such an existence will transcend the limits of our present one in countless and unimagined ways, but earth will still be our home wherever else we may go, and we will be at home there, not in exile from heaven, for heaven will have come down to earth.

The city of God

In Revelation 21 the new Jerusalem, the Holy City, is not buildings but people, the population of heaven, millions coming to inherit the earth, standing on that last great day in the full beauty of their resurrection state, fully redeemed at last.

Here, in the metaphor of a city, we are also reminded that we are made to live with others, to be social and not solitary, united and not alienated, in a home that is permanent and not transient. Since the fall, the city has been so often the symbol of arrogance and competition, exploitation and greed, poverty and lawlessness. Jerusalem itself had a poor history, and was a feeble image of this final reality. But this is the new Jerusalem, the bride in her wedding dress, and this is the new humanity in Christ, human beings in the image of God, the likeness of Christ, the beauty of holiness.

To say the state is permanent is not of course to say it is static, only that it will not decline or collapse or end in failure. The city is not a place of paralysis, but progress, a place where the arts and the sciences, and learning of all sorts, and developments of every kind thrive and grow. In the final state we shall be in eternal growth and development and progress, continuing the creation project in ways un-thought of and unimaginable in this and perhaps in other worlds.

We must never turn biblical faith and the Christian religion into a kind of National Trust idyll where we become most fully Christians in serenity and solitude rather than in the challenge and opportunity of city life day by day. God is not a National Trust asset: he is the God of the city as well as the countryside, the crowds as well as the lonely places, our building projects and engineering feats and laboratory research, as well as our gardens and holiday walks.

The final word

> And I heard a loud voice from the throne saying, 'Look! God's dwelling-place is now among the people, and he will dwell with them. They will be his people, and God himself will be with them and be their God.'
>
> (Revelation 21:3)

We shall spend eternity working out, and also working in, the implications of that verse. Whatever else it means, all that we do and everywhere we go, we will be aware of God being with us in a new way.

Perhaps we shall have festival times when thousands of us gather together, perhaps solitary times when we walk alone with our thoughts, but at all times we will be able to commune with God, to continue the conversation, to be speaker and listener by turns, and to know that our happiness will never end. We shall have God in partnership in all the tricky problems or major projects we undertake, and we shall have his glory and his smile as the goal of all we do.

Where is the temple?

When the Jews spoke of the new earth, they often spoke of the temple that would dominate it: a temple larger and more beautiful than Solomon's ever was. The prophet Ezekiel used that picture too. For the Jews, the temple at Jerusalem was the dwelling place of God, the centre of the earth, the meeting place of earth and heaven. There could be no vision of heaven without these things, and therefore their vision of the new world had this at its centre: the temple of Yahweh.

John, however, goes one better and says of the City of God, the new Jerusalem, that it was *all* temple: 'I did not see a temple in the city, because the Lord God Almighty and the Lamb are its temple' (Revelation 21:22). Even John's Gentile readers were used to cities that had temples; indeed, they would have thought a city without a temple to be a very strange thing in that ancient world. But here John's readers are shown that the *people* of God's future are his temple, and that his relationship with them, nearer and clearer and more immediate than ever, will be all that the temple ever symbolized and sought to express.

In Revelation 21 heaven is presented as a city come down to earth to remind us of our place in the new world, our connectedness, our ever-developing gifts, talents and community, and our future in carrying on God's creation project. But the city is all temple, to assure us that all we do will be worship, everywhere we go will be with God, and everything we do will be priestly as well as kingly: we will be kings and priests unto God, whose image we are and whose Son has redeemed both us and all worlds.

All city, all garden, all temple!

Then the angel showed me the river of the water of life, as clear as crystal, flowing from the throne of God and of the Lamb down the middle of the great street of the city. On each side of the river stood the tree of life, bearing twelve crops of fruit, yielding its fruit every month. And the leaves of the tree are for the healing of the nations. No longer will there be any curse. The throne of God and of the Lamb will be in the city, and his servants will serve him. They will see his face, and his name will

be on their foreheads. There will be no more night. They will
not need the light of a lamp or the light of the sun, for the Lord
God will give them light. And they will reign for ever and ever.
(Revelation 22:1–5)

Revelation 22 takes us from the city to the garden or, we might
say, it makes the city a garden city. The ancient world commonly
used the figure of a garden: the very word 'paradise' was the
Persian word for garden. Here, perhaps, the approach to
the city is by means of a garden. Again, of course, we are
dealing with the concept, not something literal and descriptive.
These symbols have meaning, and it is their meaning that is
the truth. The signs, symbols and pictures all fall short of that
final truth which will be more wonderful and varied than
anything we can imagine.

There have been all sorts of utopias, from classical to
communist, and they have all disappointed those who expected
them. Here we have the picture of a new Eden, and it will not
disappoint. Its central feature is a river flowing with the water
of life. Eden had a tree of life, but this Eden has a river of life,
and what is symbolized by both is the shared life of God. In
fact, this river seems to have trees of life on either side of it
whose leaves are for the healing of the nations. You may say,
'Why should there be leaves of healing when there will be no
sickness?' But this is a picture whose details should not be
pressed like that.

Its message is that there will be no sickness or pain or death
there, because the life of God, the life of the Spirit, the life of
activity and adoration, creativity and rest, joy and peace, is
constantly and freely available, like the trees fruiting in their
seasons and the waters flowing without cessation. As the next
verses say, there will be no curse there, only blessing, no night,
only day, no humiliation and disappointment, only everlasting

reign in an everlasting creation. This world will be for ever peopled by sons and daughters of God, fully in his image, a royal family of human beings.

Jesus' headquarters

Above all, 'The throne of God and of the Lamb will be in the city, and his servants will serve him' (Revelation 22:3). Jesus will have his headquarters there. Humanity will find its true goal and freedom and satisfaction in obedience to God and in communion with him. Notice that it is 'the throne of God and of the Lamb' at the centre: it is distinctly and centrally Christian; this is not any and every vision of heaven. The image is not neutral as a garden, but specific as a throne, an occupied throne, whose occupancy is exclusively 'God and the Lamb', that is, the Father and the Son. Heaven is not heaven without Jesus Christ at the centre: the Son of God who loved us and gave himself for us.

We should not miss the fact that we also have here the Holy Spirit in the image of the river flowing from the throne, communicating the power and goodness of God. Salvation is always the Spirit's work in us, just as redemption is the Son's work for us. All that God does in us he does through the Spirit. The Father decrees salvation, the Son accomplishes it, and the Spirit applies it.

Taxi! Taxi! Come Lord Jesus!

Chapter 22 ends with a repeated reassurance and a call:

> The angel said to me, 'These words are trustworthy and true. The Lord, the God who inspires the prophets, sent his angel to show his servants the things that must soon take place.'

'Look, I am coming soon! Blessed is the one who keeps the words of the prophecy written in this scroll.' . . .

'Look, I am coming soon! My reward is with me, and I will give to each person according to what they have done. I am the Alpha and the Omega, the First and the Last, the Beginning and the End . . .'

'Yes, I am coming soon.'

Amen. Come, Lord Jesus.

(Revelation 22:6–7, 12–13, 20)

The phrase in verse 6, 'the things that must soon take place', contains the Greek word for 'soon', which is *tachei*. It sounds very like 'taxi', doesn't it? And that is no bad way to end this book. As Eugene Peterson notes in his brilliant book on Revelation, *Reversed Thunder*,

> The tone of the Greek word is caught in English by 'Taxi! Taxi!' When we hail a taxi we summon a driver and his vehicle to tend our immediate need to get somewhere. We shout, get in, and are on our way . . . no delay is anticipated. 'Taxi!'
>
> John says that the Great Event is 'taxi', that Christ is coming 'taxi', that every prayer that prays come Lord Jesus, Our Father in heaven Your kingdom come, is a call for 'taxi'. And as the Coming is always near, the Event is always at the door, the taxi has done its U turn and is sweeping down on us. The One who ascended up on high is coming again.
>
> And that means that everything that St. John writes is immediately relevant. Nothing is held back for future relevance.[3]

It is all relevant right now, we are on the way right now, let us keep our sights on what we are right now, and what we shall be in God's future.

He who testifies to these things says, 'Yes, I am coming soon.'
Amen. Come, Lord Jesus.
(Revelation 22:20)

Notes

Preface

1. Isaac Watts, 'When I Survey the Wondrous Cross' (1707).

1. Our place in God's eternal plan

1. Graham Johnston, *Preaching to a Postmodern World: A Guide to Reaching Twenty-First-Century Listeners* (Baker, 2001), p. 136.
2. Ibid., p. 82.
3. Ibid., p. 82.
4. P. T. Forsyth, *The Person and Place of Jesus Christ* (Independent Press, 1961), p. 271.
5. Os Guinness, *The Gravedigger File: Papers on the Subversion of the Modern Church* (IVP, 1983), pp. 56–57.
6. Richard Foster, 'Becoming Like Christ', *Knowing & Doing*, Spring 2003.

2. We have been set apart for God

1. John White, *The Fight: A Practical Handbook for Christian Living* (IVP, 1976), p. 179.
2. J. I. Packer, *Keep in Step with the Spirit: Finding Fullness in Our Walk with God* (IVP, 1984), pp. 96, 97.

3. J. I. Packer, *Knowing God* (Hodder & Stoughton, 1977), p. 17.

4. John Stott, *The Cross of Christ* (IVP, 1986), p. 159.

5. Henry F. Lyte, 'Praise, My Soul, the King of Heaven' (1834).

6. J. I. Packer, *God's Words* (IVP, 1981), p. 178.

7. C. J. H. Wright, *Living as the People of God: The Relevance of Old Testament Ethics* (IVP, 1983), pp. 26–28.

8. Packer, *God's Words*, p. 178.

9. Eugene Peterson, *The Jesus Way: A Conversation in Following Jesus* (Hodder & Stoughton, 2009), p. 128.

3. We are united to Christ for ever

1. Rory Shiner, 'Union with Christ', *The Briefing*, 1 June 2011; see also Rory Shiner, *One Forever: The Transforming Power of Being in Christ* (Matthias Media, 2012).

2. John Calvin, *Institutes of the Christian Religion*, tr. F. L. Battles (SCM, 1961), 4.17.1.

3. Millard J. Erickson, *Christian Theology* (Baker, 1986), pp. 952–953.

4. Robert Letham, *Union with Christ: In Scripture, History, and Theology* (P&R, 2011), pp. 1–7.

5. Anthony A. Hoekema, *Saved by Grace* (Eerdmans, 1989), p. 60.

4. The down-to-earth God

1. Augustine, *De Trinitate*, 1.7.

2. John White, *Excellence in Leadership* (IVP, 1986), pp. 20–21.

3. H. Blamires, *On Christian Truth* (SPCK, 1983), p. 71.

4. See http://bbwarfield.com/works/sermons-and-addresses/the-example-of-the-incarnation.

5. Quoted in B. B. Warfield, *The Person and Work of Christ* (P&R, 1970), p. 564.

6. John Stott's final sermon at Keswick Convention, 2007; see also http://www.cslewisinstitute.org/Becoming_More_Like_Christ_Stott.

7. Eugene Peterson, *Christ Plays in Ten Thousand Places: A Conversation in Spiritual Theology* (Hodder & Stoughton, 2005), p. 86.
8. Adapted from Jack Canfield and Jacqueline Miller (eds.), *Heart at Work* (McGraw-Hill, 1996); see also http://storiesforpreaching.com/category/sermonillustrations/significance.

5. This is your life: the Sermon on the Mount

1. J. B. Phillips, *Letters to Young Churches* (Geoffrey Bles, 1948), Preface.
2. Leon Morris, *The Gospel According to Matthew* (Eerdmans/IVP, 1992), p. 297.
3. R. T. Kendall, *Total Forgiveness* (Hodder & Stoughton, 2001); R. T Kendall, with Julia Fisher, *Tales of Total Forgiveness* (Hodder & Stoughton, 2004); R. T. Kendall, *Totally Forgiving Ourselves* (Hodder & Stoughton, 2007). For an advanced and brilliant theological treatment of forgiveness at personal and international levels, see *Exclusion and Embrace: A Theological Exploration of Identity, Otherness, and Reconciliation* by Croatian theologian Miroslav Volf (Abingdon Press, 1996).

6. The Suffering Servant and suffering Christians

1. From a sermon by Ken Matthews at Jesmond Parish Church, Newcastle, 23 December 2001; see http://printandaudio.org.uk/app/explore/resources/church/jpc/page/5/sort/date/direction/asc/resource/1069/title/the-wise-men.
2. Karen H. Jobes, *1 Peter* (Baker, 2005), p. 195.
3. Tertullian, *Apologeticus*, ch. 50.
4. See http://www.desiringgod.org/articles/being-mocked-the-essence-of-christs-work-not-muhammads.
5. Thomas A. Smail, *The Forgotten Father* (Hodder & Stoughton, 1987), p. 45.

6. David Garrison, *A Wind in the House of Islam* (Wigtake, 2015).

7. Craig S. Keener, *Acts: An Exegetical Commentary, Volume 1* (Baker, 2012), p. 582.

8. Murray J. Harris, *The Second Epistle to the Corinthians*, NIGTC (Eerdmans, 2005), p. 472.

9. *First Clement, Early Christian Writings*, tr. J. B. Lightfoot, 1 *Clem* 5:5 (see http://www.earlychristianwritings.com/text/1clement-lightfoot.html).

7. The Spirit of God

1. Isaac Watts, 'When I Survey the Wondrous Cross' (1707).

2. J. C. Ryle, *Holiness: Its Nature, Hindrances, Difficulties and Roots* (Evangelical Press, 2004), p. 16.

3. Craig Brian Larson, *Perfect Illustrations: For Every Topic and Occasion* (Tyndale House, 2002), p. 259.

4. C. S. Lewis, *Letters to Malcolm: Chiefly on Prayer* (Harcourt, Brace and World, 1963), p. 93.

5. David E. Garland, *Colossians, Philemon* (Zondervan, 1998), p. 244.

6. C. S. Lewis, *Mere Christianity* (MacMillan, 1960), pp. 95–96.

7. John Stott, *The Message of Galatians*, The Bible Speaks Today (IVP, 1993), p. 116.

8. The Word of God

1. Victor Shepherd, 'Three Wise Gentiles and a Jewish Infant': sermon, January 1998; see http://victorshepherd.ca/three-wise-gentiles-and-a-jewish-infant/.

2. Derek Kidner, *Psalms 1 – 72*, Tyndale Old Testament Commentary (IVP, 1973), p. 109.

3. See Robert J. Banks, *Paul's Idea of Community: The Early House Churches in Their Cultural Setting* (Paternoster, 1980), p. 74.

4. Donald G. Barnhouse, *Let Me Illustrate* (Revell, 1994), in the section on the Bible.

9. The place of prayer

1. Eugene Peterson, *Life at Its Best: A Guidebook for the Pilgrim Life* (Zondervan, 2002), pp. 266–267.
2. John Calvin, *Institutes of the Christian Religion*, tr. F. L. Battles (SCM, 1961), 1.8.17.
3. David F. Wells, 'Prayer: Rebelling against the Status Quo', in Ralph D. Winter and Steven C. Hawthorne (eds.), *Perspectives on the World Christian Movement: A Reader* (William Carey Library, 1999), pp. 142–144.
4. John Piper, *Let the Nations Be Glad* (IVP, 1993), p. 41.

10. The people of God

1. Howard A. Snyder, *Community of the King* (IVP, 1978), p. 69.

11. Facing the contradictions in our society

1. D. A. Carson, *The Gospel According to John* (IVP, 1991), p. 565.
2. Gary M. Burge, *John* (Zondervan, 2000), pp. 448–449.

12. Facing the contradictions within ourselves

1. Charles Durham, *Temptation: Help for Struggling Christians* (Scripture Union, 1984), pp. 17–18.
2. Steve Farrar, *Finishing Strong: Going the Distance for Your Family* (Multnomah, 1995), p. 72.
3. C. S. Lewis, *Mere Christianity* (Collins, 1984), p. 123.
4. Cornelius Plantinga, Jr, *Not the Way It's Supposed to Be: A Breviary of Sin* (Eerdmans, 1996), p. 53.
5. Guy Brandon, *Just Sex: Is It Ever Just Sex?* (IVP, 2009).
6. R. T. France, *The Gospel of Matthew*, NICNT (Eerdmans, 2007), p. 204.
7. Lois Mowday Rabey, *The Snare: Understanding Emotional and Sexual Entanglements* (Navpress, 1988), pp. 95–100.
8. Gordon MacDonald, *The Life God Blesses: Weathering the Storms of Life* (Thomas Nelson, 1997), pp. 121–122.

9. J. I. Packer, *Keep in Step with the Spirit* (IVP, 1984), p. 110.

10. Ibid., p. 35.

11. Ibid., p. 223.

12. F. F. Bruce, *The Epistle to the Galatians* (Paternoster Press, 1982), p. 245.

13. The return with Christ

1. H. Ridderbos, *Paul: An Outline of His Theology* (SPCK, 1977), p. 488.

2. http://europe.newsweek.com/qa-anglican-bishop-n-t-wright-resurrection-86227.

3. C. S. Lewis, 'The Weight of Glory', in *Transposition and Other Addresses* (Geoffrey Bles, 1949), p. 28.

14. Christlike at last!

1. http://www.thetimes.co.uk/tto/opinion/obituaries/article2085567.ece. Dorothy Clarke Wilson recounts the same experience in *Ten Fingers for God* (Paul Brand Publishing, 1996).

2. Craig S. Keener, *Revelation* (Zondervan, 2000), p. 485.

3. Eugene H. Peterson, *Reversed Thunder: The Revelation of John and the Praying Imagination* (Harper SanFrancisco, 1991), p. 190.

KESWICK MINISTRIES

Our purpose

Keswick Ministries is committed to the spiritual renewal of God's people for his mission in the world.

God's purpose is to bring his blessing to all the nations of the world. That promise of blessing, which touches every aspect of human life, is ultimately fulfilled through the life, death, resurrection, ascension and future return of Christ. All of the people of God are called to participate in his missionary purposes, wherever he may place them. The central vision of Keswick Ministries is to see the people of God equipped, encouraged and refreshed to fulfil that calling, directed and guided by God's Word in the power of his Spirit, for the glory of his Son.

Our priorities

Keswick Ministries seeks to serve the local church through:

- **Hearing God's Word**: the Scriptures are the foundation for the church's life, growth and mission, and Keswick Ministries is committed to preach and teach God's Word in a way that is faithful to Scripture and relevant to Christians of all ages and backgrounds.
- **Becoming like God's Son**: from its earliest days the Keswick movement has encouraged Christians to live godly lives in the power of the Spirit, to grow in Christlikeness and to live under his lordship in every area of life. This is God's will for his people in every culture and generation.
- **Serving God's mission**: the authentic response to God's Word is obedience to his mission, and the inevitable result of Christlikeness is sacrificial service. Keswick

Ministries seeks to encourage committed discipleship in family life, work and society, and energetic engagement in the cause of world mission.

Our ministry

- **Keswick: the event**. Every summer the town of Keswick hosts a three-week Convention, which attracts some 15,000 Christians from the UK and around the world. The event provides Bible teaching for all ages, vibrant worship, a sense of unity across generations and denominations, and an inspirational call to serve Christ in the world. It caters for children of all ages and has a strong youth and young adult programme. And it all takes place in the beautiful Lake District – a perfect setting for rest, recreation and refreshment.

- **Keswick: the movement**. For 140 years the work of Keswick has impacted churches worldwide, and today the movement is underway throughout the UK, as well as in many parts of Europe, Asia, North America, Australia, Africa and the Caribbean. Keswick Ministries is committed to strengthen the network in the UK and beyond, through prayer, news, pioneering and cooperative activity.

- **Keswick resources**. Keswick Ministries is producing a growing range of books and booklets based on the core foundations of Christian life and mission. It makes Bible teaching available through free access to mp3 downloads, and the sale of DVDs and CDs. It broadcasts online through Clayton TV and annual BBC Radio 4 services. In addition to the summer Convention, Keswick Ministries is hoping to develop other teaching and training events in the coming years.

Our unity

The Keswick movement worldwide has adopted a key
Pauline statement to describe its gospel inclusivity:
'for you are all one in Christ Jesus' (Galatians 3:28). Keswick
Ministries works with evangelicals from a wide variety of
church backgrounds, on the understanding that they share
a commitment to the essential truths of the Christian faith
as set out in our statement of belief.

Our contact details

Mail: Keswick Ministries, Keswick Convention Centre,
Skiddaw Street, Keswick, CA12 4BY, England
T: 017687 80075
E: info@keswickministries.org
W: www: keswickministries.org

Several hundred studies, written and spoken, by Peter Lewis on many Bible books are available at **www.peterlewis.cornerstonechurch.org.uk.**